George could not go another step. "We will stop at the next creek and wait for morning," he ordered his Indian guide, who was fifteen or twenty paces ahead of him.

The Indian made no reply and kept walking. They broke out of the trees and began to cross a meadow. It was quite light because of the snow on the ground. They could see where they were going for once instead of stumbling among the thickets of the deep forest. George thought this would be a good place to stop. He called, "Find water. We will stop here."

Suddenly, the Indian turned, bringing his gun up as he did. He took dead aim at George and fired.

Duel in the Wilderness

By Karin Clafford Farley

Colonial Williamsburg

The Colonial Williamsburg Foundation
Williamsburg, Virginia

© 1995 by Karin Clafford Farley
All rights reserved. Published 2004
First edition published 1995
Printed in China
Fifth printing 2004

Cover art by George Gaadt

ISBN 0-87935-130-6

*Colonial Williamsburg is a registered trade
name of The Colonial Williamsburg
Foundation, a not-for-profit educational
institution.*

The Colonial Williamsburg Foundation
P.O. Box 1776
Williamsburg, VA 23187-1776
www.colonialwilliamsburg.org

For Kendall, Taryn, and Alex Farley

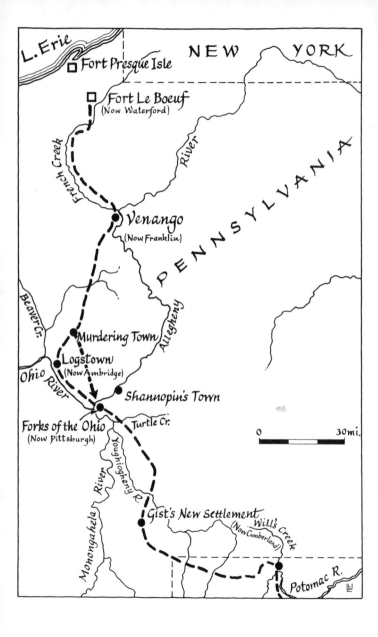

Chapter One

The Mission

*Wednesday, October 31, 1753—Williamsburg,
Colony and Dominion of Virginia*

The young soldier reached into the pocket of his coat and pulled out the letter with the broken wax seal on the back. He read it all the way through again even though he had memorized the brief message since it had been delivered early that morning.

Major Washington, Esquire,

> You are ordered to present yourself
> before the Governor and the Council at
> the Capitol Building at Noon today.
> > Robert Dinwiddie

George bit his thin lower lip as he studied the few words on the paper, searching for some meaning he might have missed. But the single sentence could not be made to reveal more. Refolding the paper, he stuffed it back into his pocket. He fixed his blue-gray eyes on the closed double doors of the Council chamber as if willing them to open. "What are they saying about me, the Governor and those principal men of

1

the colony deciding my fate in there? Why don't they call me before them and get it over with? What are they debating about? I can just hear one of those overstuffed great landowners saying, 'What? George Washington? Why, he is no gentleman. He toils for his living with his hands, a surveyor of land. A person of no importance. Never will be. A young upstart. How dare he ask that a mission of such importance be entrusted to him?'"

George's face burned as he thought of the embarrassment he was about to suffer before the Council. "I will look like a fool. Why did I listen to Colonel Fairfax and offer my services to the Governor? I must have taken leave of my senses. I will never thrust myself so boldly forward again."

Yet even as he blamed himself, George could not quite put out the fire that burned in his heart. If he could be appointed to carry out this mission, he dreamed, then he might become an important man in the colony. Maybe he could realize his father's ambition to regain a place for the Washingtons at the Council table in there.

He glanced again at the closed doors. Sighing impatiently, he resigned himself to a long time of waiting. He folded his long frame and forced himself to sit on one of the leather-covered square chairs in the Council chamber anteroom.

But the chair became an anxious seat, and

George again began pacing up and down, up and down the narrow anteroom. He tried to relieve the turmoil in his mind by looking out the window. Below him, crowds of people, horses, carts, and carriages drifted up and down dusty Duke of Gloucester Street. His back was to the Council chamber when the doors opened and Nathaniel Walthoe, the clerk of the Council, came out to speak to him in a nervous whisper. "Major Washington, His Honour, the Governor, and the members of the Council would be pleased if you would come in now."

George's heart began to pound. His naturally pale skin faded beneath his brown hair caught in a queue at the back of his neck. For one frantic moment, he feared his powerful legs might not hold him if he tried to take a step because they seemed to have turned to jelly.

He had learned in childhood to be wary of people, so he prepared to face the Governor and the Council members by withdrawing into himself. He arranged the muscles of his slightly smallpox-marked face into a mask to hide his feelings. His large fists were clenched at his sides, but he forced them open. He pulled himself up to his full six-foot, three-inch height and threw back his broad shoulders. Holding his head high, he strode into the Council chamber, his boots sounding a slow, even march on the wide planks of the floor.

Mr. Walthoe said, "Your Honour, esteemed

members of the Council, Major George Washington, adjutant for the southern district of the colony and dominion of Virginia."

George stood at attention while the secretary introduced him. Then, extending his right leg forward as was the custom, he bowed deeply to the Governor and the Council members.

Robert Dinwiddie, the royal lieutenant governor, sat in a carved wood and cane armchair topped with a crown at the far end of the large oval table. The table itself was covered with a brightly woven turkey carpet littered with quill pens, inkwells, and papers. Only eight members of the twelve-member Council were present. They sat in identical chairs, except for the crown, on either side of the table. George stood alone at the open end. No one smiled or attempted to put George at ease, not even his friend, Colonel William Fairfax.

George fixed his eyes on the Governor; they never wavered. His muscles never twitched. His mouth, set in a firm, thin line, never quivered, except once. As George looked at the Governor, he could not help seeing him as a fat, melting candle. His red face drooped down onto his double chins which met his fallen chest which had slipped onto his overhanging stomach. George felt one corner of his mouth curve up as he fought back a grin.

In spite of his appearance, Robert Dinwiddie was no fool. His sharp blue eyes narrowed,

4

almost disappearing into his fat face as he studied the young man before him. "Major Washington, I have informed the Council members of your offer to act as a diplomatic messenger to carry a letter to the French commander and learn by what right he has come into His Majesty's lands beyond the Allegheny Mountains on the River Ohio," he said in a thick Scottish accent.

Before Governor Dinwiddie could say more, one of the elderly Council members struggled to his feet. "Your Honour, I must protest! When you said the Major here was a younger brother of the late Major Lawrence Washington, I did not realize how much younger. Why, he is but a boy! How can you think of sending him on such a delicate mission to the French? We need a man of experience! Mature judgment! I'll wager he has not yet reached his majority. He would have to ask his mother's permission to go!"

Laughter broke out around the table.

Burning under such cruel joking at his expense, George felt his control over his fiery temper slip away from him, and he did not care. Anger flashed in his eyes. He knew he should not speak while standing at attention, but the words were out before he could stop them. "I turned twenty-one early this year, Sir!"

His protest went unheeded as another councillor joined in. "Your Honour, I agree. I did not realize when we confirmed your appointment of Mr. Washington to replace his late brother as adjutant that he was not nearer in age and experience to the three other adjutants of the dominion's militia."

This time George caught a shake of the head and a warning look from his friend, Colonel William Fairfax. He struggled to control his temper by clamping his teeth over the inside of his lower lip until he tasted blood.

Robert Dinwiddie answered their protests. "Gentlemen, you know I have offered this mission to several other older, more qualified men. They have all found reasons to decline it. The Major here is a military man. We need a military man to spy—ah—er—assess the French buildup of forces in the Ohio country."

Colonel Fairfax interrupted. "Gentlemen, I have known Major Washington for many years. His brother Lawrence was my son-in-law. George is like a second son to me. Since the age of fifteen, he has earned his own way as a licensed surveyor for this colony and has the reputation for being one of the most skillful. He has traveled many times to the frontier in the course of his work. He is used to the hard, out-of-doors life."

"But has he ever crossed the mountains to Logstown or Murdering Town?" someone shouted out.

Colonel Fairfax answered by asking his own question. "Who has crossed the mountains? That is a dark and mysterious land to us. The Indian tribes have allowed some traders in; men who are useful to them. Sometimes we have coaxed a few of the Indians to the edge of the wilderness to give them presents, to assure them we are their brothers. But no high official of the government has gone beyond the mountains. Not from this colony nor any other that I know of. Now this fine young man, one of our own Virginia militia adjutants, has volunteered to undertake this critical task, and you question, Sir? Could you endure the hardships of such a journey, Sir? Certainly I could not. His youth is what recommends him most. I say we engage him."

But the councillor was not to be put off. "Last year, His Honour tried to send a letter to the French by Trader William Trent, a man of long experience in the wilderness. Even Trent was afraid to go north of Logstown toward Lake Erie where the French are known to be. Traders have been taken prisoner or killed, their goods taken, and they themselves sent to gaol in Canada. Every day more Indians ally themselves to the French, who reward them for killing Englishmen. If Major Washington is like a son to you, how can you suggest he make a journey from which he has so little hope of returning?"

Gaol in cold Canada? The very thought made George shiver. No, no, he told himself, he would be a diplomat, not a trader. English traders might be imprisoned, but not diplomats. At this very moment, William Keppel, Earl of Albemarle and the official royal governor of Virginia, was the English ambassador to the French court. Yet he could not take such heart about the Indians being rewarded for killing Englishmen. A vivid memory crowded his mind. He was on a surveying trip on the upper Potomac River and he stopped for the night at Trader Thomas Cresap's outpost. While there, he met an Iroquois war party, friendly to Cresap, returning up the Warrior's Path from a raid on the Cherokees. All night long they danced to their pounding drums and the rattle of gourds. Five years had passed, but George could feel his excitement as if it were yesterday.

Colonel Fairfax continued to speak to the Council. "I have great trust in Major Washington, as does my esteemed cousin, Lord Fairfax. Major Washington is a great favorite of his lordship's."

At the mention of Thomas, Lord Fairfax, to whose grandfather King Charles I had granted the largest tract of land in Virginia, the entire Shenandoah Valley, all discussion among the Council members abruptly ended. His lordship rarely left Greenwood, his estate in the remote Shenandoah Valley. But he made his power as the wealthiest man and highest ranking nobleman in the colony felt through his kinsman, Colonel William Fairfax.

Governor Dinwiddie drew attention back

to himself. He did not look at the Council members. Instead, he studied George intently. "Just so there is no misunderstanding, do you know what I am asking?"

George made no effort to reply. His eyes remained fixed on the Governor's face, and he tried not to blink.

"To deliver this letter we would send in the King's name, you would have to cross the Alleghenies to Venango or heaven knows where to find the French commander. You would be gone at least a month, for there are no roads beyond Winchester, as you know. Snow and rain will be coming to the high country. And if you do make contact with the French, they no doubt will smile in your face, shrug their shoulders in that confounded Gallic way they have, send me a charming letter in return, and have one of their agents put a knife in your back some dark night. That is the mission we speak of. Do you still wish to volunteer?"

George could feel the eyes of Queen Anne boring into his back from her portrait hanging on the wall behind him. "I am ready, Sir, to serve faithfully my King and country in any way I can."

What else could he say? No man of pride could withdraw his offer of service after appearing before the Council. Any hope he had to advance himself and maybe one day sit on this very Council as his grandfather had would be cut off forever. Colonel Fairfax had urged him to volunteer as a chance to achieve those ends. He knew George was ambitious. To withdraw now would mean disgrace. "I am strong. I am hard enough. I can make it, winter or no," he thought.

Robert Dinwiddie looked around the table. "Very well, then. If there be no more discussion?" Each Council member nodded yea. "Then I, the Honourable Robert Dinwiddie, Esquire, lieutenant governor and commander in chief of the colony and dominion of Virginia, chancellor and vice admiral of the same, appoint you, George Washington, Esquire, one of the adjutants of the troops and forces in the colony of Virginia, to this mission this thirty-first day of October in the twenty-seventh year of the reign of His Majesty, George the Second, King of Great Britain, in the year of our Lord, 1753."

George could hardly believe Governor Dinwiddie was saying the words he had dreamed of hearing. It was official, the mission was his. At last his chance to be somebody had come. He raised his arm in salute, making known his acceptance.

Governor Dinwiddie gave him his orders. "I direct you to travel to Logstown on the River Ohio and learn where the French forces are. Then betake yourself to such place. Speak only to the highest ranking officer in the region and give him this letter I now entrust to you." Governor Dinwiddie waved the heavy folded paper with a great wax seal toward George. "Do not let him put you off. Insist upon an immediate answer.

"But before you leave Logstown, introduce yourself to an important representative of the Six Nations named Tanacharison, otherwise known as Half King, and any other leaders as you find. Tell them of your mission and ask them to provide you with a large escort of their young men to ensure your safety. These tribes are friendly to the British. See that they continue to be our brothers. They must not ally themselves with the French," he warned.

An army of warriors! George imagined himself riding up before the French commander at the head of hundreds of Indians. What a grand moment that would be! The vision made him almost dizzy with power. He pulled his mind back to the Governor, who continued to talk on.

"Now we are aware, although you have had experience on the frontier, you have never penetrated so deeply as Logstown. Therefore, you are to proceed to Will's Creek first and deliver my request to one Christopher Gist that he act as your guide."

George recognized the name of Gist, the explorer, and he was troubled by it. He tried to speak, but Dinwiddie's face became flushed as he issued the last instructions to George.

"When you do find the French commander, you are to ask him straight out why he made prisoners of British traders and sent them to Canada, and why Trader John Frazier was driven from his house at Venango.

"Finally, Major Washington, I warn you to make haste. Return immediately back with the reply of the French to my letter! It is of the utmost importance. Do you understand what you are to do?"

"Sir, who is to be in command—Mr. Gist or me?"

"You are in command, Major, in all things."

George knew what those words meant. If the mission failed, he would be held responsible; his career in public service would be ended, certainly. But if he succeeded, the glory would be his and his future assured. The next month would decide his destiny.

"Do you have any questions, Major?" asked the Governor.

Questions? George had a thousand questions tumbling around inside his brain, but he could not put them into words now. He only cared that the mission was his. He, George Washington, was in command. He felt a surge of pride, and it took all his iron self-control to keep from smiling broadly.

"Very well. Here is my letter. Guard it well. Here are your passport and your commission from me. Also your written instructions. Study them carefully. Oh yes, and a voucher to the Receiver General to advance you one hundred fifty pounds to defray your expenses for the expedition, and my letter to Mr. Gist. I wish you

Godspeed, Major." The eight Council members were silent.

Mr. Walthoe nodded to the doorkeeper, who hurried to open the double doors of the Council chamber, signaling George the Council's business with him was at an end.

"A moment, Major Washington." Colonel Fairfax pushed back his chair from the table, stood up, and walked toward George. "On behalf of the Council," he said loudly, his eyes sweeping the table, "We will remember you in our prayers, and we thank you for volunteering to carry out this important task."

"Thank you, Sir." George was grateful for his friend's efforts in gaining this commission for him.

"Take care, George, take great care. The family looks forward to having you with us at Christmas," said Colonel Fairfax.

"I will do my best to be there."

"I have great faith in your best, m'boy." They shook hands warmly.

George felt a twinge of annoyance at being called boy though he knew his friend meant it kindly. He went to the open doors. Turning, he bowed to the Governor and the Council in farewell.

When the doors were closed, shutting him out once more, Governor Dinwiddie's words "Return immediately back" echoed in his ears. He could not waste a moment. Tucking the papers entrusted to him into his coat pocket, he hurried down the stairs. A doorkeeper opened the door of the Capitol and made a bow.

George ran across the grass and through the gate in the brick wall surrounding the Capitol. After untying the reins of his horse, he paused for a moment for one last look back at the three-story brick building that represented the King of England in Virginia. "I'll show those old grandees with their mansions and their coats of arms. They do not really expect that I will return. But I'll be back. I'll show them what a boy can do." He mounted up. Spurring his horse into a gallop on Francis Street, he headed west.

Chapter Two

The Odyssey Begins

Thursday, November 1, 1753—Fredericksburg,
Colony and Dominion of Virginia

George sagged in his saddle as he rode into Fredericksburg. Each step his horse took jarred him to his bones. He had traveled a hundred miles in less than day with only a fitful night's sleep on the floor of a tavern.

This town should have been his home for he had lived across the Rappahannock River at Ferry Farm from the time he was six years old until he was thirteen. His widowed mother, three younger brothers, and his sister still lived here. He was tempted to take a little time to inspect the current condition of the three pieces of property in the town that his father had willed to him. But, again, he heard Dinwiddie's words in his mind, "Return immediately back." The business of the mission and the mission only was all he could concern himself with.

He needed an interpreter to deal with the French, and he remembered hearing from his brother, Jack, that a man who gave French lessons had moved into the town. Knowing the best place to find out about the man was to ask at a tavern, he guided his horse toward the largest one in town across from the main wharf on the river.

Finding it still in business, he dismounted in front of the modest frame building painted yellow. No one was about but a servant girl who was sweeping the front steps. "I wish to see the innkeeper," George demanded. The girl scurried away without a word.

Soon an older man in shirt sleeves appeared. "You wish to see me, Sir?" he asked timidly.

In his eagerness to be on with his mission, George suddenly realized his curtness was scaring the man and his servant. He spoke more patiently. "Innkeeper, I seek a Dutch gentleman I was told lives hereabouts. Do you know him or have you heard talk of him?"

The innkeeper was most eager to please a possible customer. "You must mean Jacob Van Braam, Sir. Arrived here but last year."

"He teaches the French language?" George asked.

"Yes, yes. The very one."

"Jacob Van Braam, you say. Where can he be found?"

"But a mile or two beyond the town."

"Which way?"

"Out the North Road. He has a little house there . . ."

George turned and hurried out the door

as the last words were spoken. He remembered from his childhood just where the innkeeper meant he could find this Van Braam. He waved his thanks.

Remounting, he headed his horse out the North Road. In a matter of minutes, he was at the house knocking on the door. George was very relieved to see that the man who answered his knock was only a few years older than he was. He had not thought until this moment what he would do if Van Braam had been old and infirm. "Mr. Van Braam? Mr. Jacob Van Braam?" George asked.

"At your service, Sir," said the young man in a heavy accent. He bowed in an elaborate manner.

"I am Major George Washington, adjutant of the colony on business for the Governor," he said, hoping the fellow would be impressed.

Jacob Van Braam stepped aside and bade George enter his poor dwelling. In one corner, some quilts lay on a rope frame. A rickety table and some backless stools were beside the hearth. The only things that caused the seedy room to look like the dwelling of a gentleman were the books on a shelf and the sword over the fireplace.

George cleared his throat. "Mr. Van Braam, I understand you know the French language well?"

"Ya, ya," Van Braam answered in Dutch, then changed to English. "Yes, I know French. I was officer in Dutch army. You want lessons in French? I'm good teacher."

George had a difficult time understanding Van Braam, and what he did understand began to sound like boasting. But he was pleased at some of what he did manage to catch. To have a man with military experience on the mission would be a great asset. George felt doubly in luck.

"I came to colonies last year," Van Braam continued nervously when George did not say anything. "I speak French good. Je parle français et je lis français et j'écris français et . . ." (I speak French and I read French and I write French).

He could have been speaking Chinese for all George understood what he was saying. "No, no, I do not want to learn French myself. I need an interpreter; someone who can understand French, translate it into English, and then translate what I say back into French. Do you think you could do that?" George spoke very slowly and loudly as if he were talking to someone hard of hearing.

Van Braam stared at him with a blank expression.

George tried again. "Mr. Van Braam, I am sent by Governor Dinwiddie to seek the French forces beyond the Allegheny Mountains. I do not speak French at all, yet I must conduct matters of diplomacy with the French. This trip will go deep into Indian country, and we will be gone at least a month."

Van Braam looked alarmed. "Indian? We not go to Quebec? Montreal?"

"No, I go beyond the mountains." George waved his arm wildly toward the west, trying to explain his purpose to Jacob Van Braam. "Can you go with me? You would be well paid." George glanced around the poor dwelling again.

Van Braam's face took on a different look at the mention of money. "How much?"

George had not thought about pay. A figure leaped into his head. "A shilling a day." He knew it was too much as the words left his lips.

"A shilling?"

"The Governor allows me no more," George said quickly to cut off any bargaining Van Braam might be thinking of.

"Ya, I go with you. No wife, no children, no work."

"How soon can you be ready? I must make haste."

"Now. I pack my things." Van Braam set to work at once pulling clothes off pegs in the logs and taking blankets and a cloak out of a leather trunk. He removed his sword from over the hearth.

George was pleased at how easily he had acquired the first member of his expedition. He had been in command less than a day.

He stepped outside Van Braam's house to take his horse down to the river to drink. As he looked across the Rappahannock toward Ferry

Farm, he felt a twinge of guilt that he should stop at the farm and tell his family where he was going. What if he never came back?

"No, I had better not," he thought. "Mother will only cry and demand I not go. It would be of no interest to my mother that this might be a great opportunity for her oldest son to become an important man in the colony—if I live to return from this journey. Maybe if Father had lived, he would have understood."

George found his memories of his father, Augustine, had faded in the ten years since his death. He shrank from thinking ill of the dead, especially his own father. But he could not deny that his father had mismanaged the inheritance his great-grandfather and grandfather had wrested from the wilderness of the New World. His father had allowed the Washingtons to slip below the circle of families whose representatives sat on the Council at Williamsburg.

Through his two oldest sons, Lawrence and Austin, George knew his father had hoped to regain a place for the Washingtons as one of the first families of Virginia. George remembered how he fired his older half-brothers with ambition and pride. Though it was beyond his means, he sent them to England to be educated. He was determined they must be gentlemen.

But that meant there was nothing left over for George, his third son, the first child of his second marriage. Reading, writing, and ciphering taught by an indentured servant or traveling teachers were good enough for him.

When George was six, Lawrence returned from England, an elegant young gentleman of twenty. George remembered how he had loved and imitated him. He learned gracious manners, swordsmanship, and, with great eagerness, military matters. For Lawrence had served under Admiral Vernon in the Cartagena campaign on the north coast of South America. When their father died, George went to live with Lawrence at Mount Vernon. Those years were the happiest of his life. Lawrence became his substitute parent.

After Lawrence's death, George's grief for his beloved half-brother, instead of shattering him, somehow steeled him to carry on in his place. He applied for Lawrence's commission as an adjutant of the Virginia militia even though he had not yet reached his twenty-first birthday and legal adulthood. Nudged by Colonel Fairfax, Governor Dinwiddie appointed him an adjutant. George found it a pleasing experience to strut around inspecting small groups of citizen-soldiers in small towns, being saluted and called "Major" by farmers and merchants twice his age. To say nothing of collecting a hundred pounds a year for such easy duties.

Now Governor Dinwiddie had given him this important trust, perhaps hoping George had the same fine qualities as his brother. But George was not Lawrence. He was not a well educated and experienced thirty-five-year-old man; he was a twenty-one-year-old boy just turning into a man. "All I can do is try," he pledged to himself.

"Major?" Jacob Van Braam broke into George's deep thoughts. "I'm ready to go."

"What? Oh good, good, Mr. Van Braam!" He pushed his family and the past from his mind. The future was all that mattered. The two young men mounted their horses and started north toward Alexandria.

After buying the supplies he thought he would need in Alexandria and Winchester, the last white man's town east of the Allegheny Mountains, George and Jacob followed the New Road out of Winchester toward Will's Creek. They led a string of many packhorses laden down with a tent, blankets, bags of cornmeal, smoked meat, jugs of brandy, guns and ammunition, medicine, tobacco, and presents for the Indians. After George made his purchases, he realized that in his inexperience he had weighted himself down with too much baggage. Handling so many horses was difficult for just two men, especially when Van Braam had no experience with wilderness travel. For the New Road was nothing but a trail sometimes hardly visible as it passed thorough muddy bottoms and across unbridged streams. George prayed he would not become lost, for he had never been this far west before on his surveying work. Yet he had to hide his uncertainty from Jacob Van Braam as he led him deeper and deeper into the woods.

George had another worry he did not share with Van Braam. Two men alone burdened with much baggage were a tempting target for thieves. George took some comfort in Jacob being a trained soldier.

It was far better than being alone. Van Braam tried to keep their spirits up with a never-ending supply of stories about his life in Europe. The way he told them in his badly broken English made George laugh. George knew Van Braam must be afraid. Yet like the soldier he once was, he tried to do anything George asked because his survival depended upon following his commander and learning the ways of the frontier as quickly as possible.

Near dusk on November 14, they came to yet another peaceful valley sheltered by steep mountainsides. Through the center rushed a small river, and on the other side was a cluster of rude cabins. George whooped, "We're here!" He thanked Providence he had managed to find his way as far as Will's Creek.

"Come on!" George urged his horse into the swift but shallow water. Van Braam followed. As they cleared the opposite bank, several men came out to meet them. Some carried guns. They squinted at the new arrivals in the fading light.

He spoke to the nearest one. "I am Major Washington on the Gov . . ." George hesitated.

When he had crossed the upper Potomac River, he was no longer in Virginia, but in the Maryland colony. "I am on the King's business," he corrected himself. "Where can I find Mr. Christopher Gist?" he asked before anyone had time to question him.

A man jerked his thumb toward the cabins. One was larger than the rest, so George assumed that would be the most likely place to find Christopher Gist. "Take care of the horses, Mr. Van Braam," he ordered, for he wanted to speak to Christopher Gist alone. They had secret business.

When he knocked at the rough-hewn door, it was opened by a man as big as himself. He was dressed in leather leggings made from animal hides and a homespun shirt. In the darkness, George could not see his face very well and thought he must be a servant. "I seek Christopher Gist," he said curtly.

"I am Christopher Gist. At your service, Sir," the man said, and made an elegant bow.

George, in turn, was astounded. "You . . . you are Christopher Gist?" He tried to make sure this was the right man, the man so respected by Governor Dinwiddie.

"Indeed I am. And may I inquire who seeks me?" he asked.

George wished the ground would open up and swallow him. He had appeared at this man's door out of the night, spoken to him as he would

24

a servant, questioned his word, and now he stood like a gaping schoolboy. He had not done even the first courtesy of introducing himself.

"I . . . I am George Washington, Major George Washington," he stammered. "I have letters for you from Governor Dinwiddie, Sir." George made an awkward bow.

"Major Washington, welcome to Will's Creek. Please come in and warm yourself. I will attend to your horse myself."

"My interpreter with the assistance of some men is already seeing to that task. My business with you is urgent, so if I may . . . ?"

"At once!" Christopher Gist stepped aside and allowed George to enter the log cabin.

"May I take your cloak, Major, and fetch you food and drink? Come, sit by my fire. I will build it up," Gist offered, with as much courtesy as would be found in the finest houses in Williamsburg.

But George waved his offer aside. Instead, he pulled out his packet of papers and unwrapped them from their oilcloth pouch. He gave the proper letter to Gist.

Christopher Gist leaned against the chimney to read it. George studied him in the firelight. He was not young like Van Braam. George estimated he was at least twice his own age. His hair was streaked with gray and his weathered face was deeply lined. Yet his manners were those of a gentleman despite his frontier-style dress.

His appearance troubled George, for he wondered how Gist could endure the trip that he himself had already found so exhausting.

"Damn!" Christopher Gist exclaimed when he had finished. "Has Dinwiddie lost his senses?"

George's heart sank.

Gist looked at George angrily. "I told Governor Dinwiddie two months ago in Williamsburg that the French have built a fort at Presque Isle on the south shore of Lake Erie. They've built a wagon road to French Creek. This gives their soldiers and supplies a clear way to the Allegheny River and the River Ohio itself. Governor Duquesne of Canada has stated publicly he is determined to have the Ohio Valley for France and he is succeeding. And all Dinwiddie does is send one lone boy . . ." Gist stopped. "One lone officer into this hostile territory to defy the old French commander, de Marin, who is backed up by hundreds of soldiers?"

George stiffened at those words. "The Governor hopes to avoid a war," he said defensively. "He has orders from London not to attack without good reason, but to try to persuade the French to withdraw peacefully."

"Avoid a war? It has already begun!" Gist ranted. "We need soldiers. Forts built. A show of strength. Or we will lose the Ohio Valley."

"I am to talk with the Indians, meet with an important man named Half King and other chiefs. Win them to our side to fight against the

French, if that should become necessary."
George repeated Governor Dinwiddie's words.

Christopher Gist looked at George, and George squirmed under his silent stare. "Major Washington, the Indians will side with whomever they think is the strongest even if it means they change sides every week. Have you not heard of Pickawillany?"

"You mean the massacre at Pickawillany?" George asked.

"Yes. The Twightwees, part of the Miami nation, as you may know them, were great friends to the English. But Governor Duquesne sent Charles Langlade and another Frenchman from Fort Detroit with two hundred forty Algonquian, Chippewa, and Ottawa allies to surprise the Twightwees and the English traders." Gist's face was very grim. "There were about four hundred Indian families at Pickawillany when I visited there two years ago. The traders had helped the Indians fortify the town. It was the strongest of all the Indian towns. Yet it fell. The cruelties were the worst I have ever heard of, and I have seen some terrible ones with my own eyes. They killed one English trader and ate his heart. Others were taken prisoner to God knows where. All of their goods were taken.

"The French made an example of Pickawillany to frighten the other tribes into siding with them, and their plan is working too well, I am afraid. What is left of the Twightwees after the massacre side with the French. Every tribe in the Ohio Valley will go the same way sooner or later unless the English show force. All this summer the tribes have been in panic. They do not understand why the English do not come to their aid. They demand guns, but the English are afraid to give them. They want a fort to protect their women and children!"

George wondered why the Governor did not tell Gist in the letter that he wanted to learn the military strength of the French before he committed Virginia troops to this struggle. And why was not Gist sent by the Governor to be in charge of this mission? The feeling of betrayal crept into George's mind. He heard Dinwiddie's words, "I have offered this mission to several other older, more qualified men who have found reasons to decline it." Governor Dinwiddie knew of this situation, if Gist spoke the truth, and he had not told George.

"Mr. Gist, the Governor has requested that you accompany me as a guide. Do you feel you cannot agree to the Governor's request as you fear for your own safety?" George spoke carefully, fearful of Gist's answer. Would he have to continue alone? Only with the help of Providence had he found his way to this English outpost. How would he find Logstown without Gist to guide him?

"Major Washington, last summer Governor Dinwiddie sent Trader William Trent on this same mission to protest and warn the French to get out of the Ohio Valley. But Trent thought it foolhardy to go north of Logstown. If traders who know the Indians, have been their friends for years, will not venture into the deep woods anymore because they risk almost certain scalping, how do you expect to reach the French—alive?"

"I know of Trent. But the governor has instructed me to ask for a large escort of Indians from tribes known to be friendly with the English. Besides, I am an emissary. I have a passport and a commission signed by Governor Dinwiddie on behalf of His Majesty. I have diplomatic immunity according to international law," George stated with confidence.

"But there is no law out here!" protested Christopher Gist. "We may claim this land and the French may claim this land, but the laws of neither country can be enforced here. There is only the law of the tomahawk. How can I make you understand that?"

Exhaustion suddenly overcame George. Two weeks of struggle on the wilderness trail to get his pack train to Will's Creek only to be told to turn around and go back? NO! His temper boiled up from deep within him, and he did not even try to hold it back.

"What do you expect me to do? Ride for home? Mr. Gist, you understand! Trader Trent is a civilian. You are a civilian. You were *requested* by the Governor to go into the wilderness and find the French. I am a soldier. I am under orders. I must carry out the charge the Governor and the Council have given to me. It is my duty regardless of the personal risks. If you cannot go with me, then I will push on alone," he said, steeling himself to carry out his order to the end.

The look on Christopher Gist's face was not one of admiration for George's brave words. He tried one last time. "I am acquainted with your older brother, a fine gentleman. Does he not know of this suicide mission you have undertaken?"

"My brother is in his grave."

Gist was silent a long time. "Major Washington, is it worth your life to continue on this hopeless mission?" Gist asked.

"I must serve my King," George answered nobly.

"You are not serving your King, you are serving the Ohio Company. You and I are being asked to risk death so men back in Williamsburg can make fat profits over our frozen bodies."

"But the governor and the Council ordered me . . ."

"You may be assured that they ordered you because most of them, and the Governor, too, are members of the Ohio Company. That is why Dinwiddie replaced Governor William Gooch. Dinwiddie would push the settlement of the Ohio lands. Right now the French are the only thing stopping their grand plans."

"I, too, am a member of the Ohio Company. I would like to see the lands settled," George stated defensively.

"And I am the chief surveyor for the company. I have fifty families signed up to move west and buy some of the two hundred thousand acres the Governor and the Council members as well as you and I own. But it is not worth my life," Gist countered.

"I will push on, Mr. Gist, with you or without you."

Finally, Gist answered in a strangely formal way. "If, in your judgment as commander of this mission, you wish to proceed, then I will serve as the Governor has requested." But again he looked with pity upon George. "I think I must go with you," he said quietly.

George sagged with relief. "When can you be ready to leave? The Governor and the Council bade me to make haste."

"I shall prepare immediately," answered Gist.

Chapter Three

The Traders

*Thursday, November 15, 1753—Will's Creek,
Colony of Maryland*

The next morning, Major George Washington commanded an expedition almost four times larger than the one he had commanded only the evening before. Besides Christopher Gist and Jacob Van Braam, Gist had persuaded four traders at Will's Creek to accompany them to handle the horses and baggage and give extra protection. Since they could not work as traders any longer because of the French, they were glad to have any work, especially since Major Washington promised to pay their wages in cash money.

As the party mounted up, Gist stayed in second position behind Major Washington, the commanding officer. But before they left the valley, George said, "Mr. Gist, I am unfamiliar with the way beyond this valley. For the good of all, I ask you to take the lead."

"Then I suggest we follow the Nemacolin Trail, Major. It is the one I use to travel to my new settlement beyond Laurel Hill."

Leaving Will's Creek, the trail led directly

westward, steadily climbing higher and higher into the Allegheny Mountains. George and Christopher Gist rode out in front. George asked, "Can you tell me something about the four men accompanying us?"

Gist seemed a bit surprised. "I can recommend them. I have known and worked with all of them."

George felt he might have unknowingly given offense again to the older man, and he hastened to correct the impression. "I completely trust your recommendations. I am deeply grateful that you were able to persuade them to come with us. I just wish to know their special abilities so I can use each person to best support this expedition."

"Well, Barnaby Currin there is from Pennsylvania. He went with me two years ago to survey the south side of the River Ohio for Virginia. He was in the Indian trade as partner with George Croghan before Croghan had thousands of pounds in trading goods stolen from him at Pickawillany. Croghan is so deeply in debt, he is in hiding from debtor's prison. Do you know Croghan, Major?"

"I know him by reputation," George answered dryly.

"Too bad you don't know him personally. The Iroquois consider him their greatest white friend. They call him 'The Buck.' I wish we had him with us now. He is a master diplomat when it comes to dealing with the Indians."

"And Mr. Jenkins?" George tried to get Gist back to the subject.

"William Jenkins is known to Governor Dinwiddie. He often uses him for a messenger. John MacQuire is an Irishman who used to work for Croghan as a trader. Henry Steward came out as a settler. Lost his family in a massacre. You need not worry, Major, all these men know the woods."

As it had almost every day since George had left Williamsburg, a rain began to fall. The horsemen plodded on, the rain running down their faces and seeping into their collars. After hours, it soaked their heavy clothing. Since there was nothing he could do about it, George tried to live with the ever-present rain. Night was almost upon them when they reached George's Creek and made camp. The tent they were to sleep in was wet. Even the pine boughs they spread under their blankets to keep them from direct contact with the mud did not help much. The frontiersmen seemed to take such conditions as a way of life. But George was vexed by the slow progress the rain caused. He had hoped with Gist as guide and his four trader friends to help, the expedition could move faster. Yet the total distance traveled that day was only eight miles, he estimated.

As they sat huddled around the campfire talking after their meal, Gist suddenly grabbed for his gun that lay close beside him at all times. Currin, Jenkins, MacQuire, and Steward did the same and then faded into the darkness. George was startled.

"What's the matter, Mr. Gist?" he whispered.

"Someone is out there."

George had heard nothing, but he reached for his gun, too.

Gist pushed him away from the circle of fire-light. "Come in with your hands up!" Gist barked an order into the night.

"Annosanah," a voice said, and an Indian stepped into the firelight. Silently, he handed Gist a piece of paper. Jenkins and Currin came back to the campfire again, but Steward and MacQuire stayed out.

Christopher Gist read the message several times. Then he looked up. "It's from my son, Nathaniel. He was returning from the Cherokees when he fell ill. He is at the mouth of the Conegocheague River. He needs my help at once." Christopher Gist started toward his horse tethered nearby.

George felt fear tingle through him. Gist must not leave the expedition. "Mr. Gist, we are on the King's business and we cannot delay. I can understand your concern for your son, and if I must go on alone, I will. But the Governor felt your presence on the expedition was neces-sary for it to have any chance of success. If we don't succeed, it may mean war . . ."

"You mean we are on Ohio Company business, don't you?" Gist interrupted. "How do you other men feel?"

"We need you, Mr. Gist," said Barnaby Currin meaningfully as he glanced at young George.

Gist turned away for a long time. Then he said, "Very well. My duty is clear. Give this man some food," he ordered.

George approached Gist, but he was already busy opening the medicine pack and writing something down on a piece of paper.

Meanwhile, the Indian messenger squatted on the ground eating with his fingers from a tin plate of food. Soon Gist came back. "Here, take this letter and this package to Nathaniel. He will know what to do."

Without a further word, the man disappeared into the forest.

"Shouldn't he wait until morning?" George protested. "How can he find his way in the night, particularly so black a night as this one?" George felt some guilt about Gist's son.

"He can find his way quite well, Major," Gist replied, as he stared into the dark forest in the direction the man had gone.

"Ya ain't known many Indians, have ya, Major?" Barnaby Currin said. George let it pass.

He pushed everyone hard including himself to carry out Governor Dinwiddie's orders. For a week, they traveled through tunnels of thick forest whose sides were made of tree trunks reinforced with matted thickets of laurel. Overhead, even the bare branches were so dense they blocked out the sky.

The mountains were high wrinkles in the earth's crust stretching for miles and miles on a north-south axis. When there was no way around them, the seven men climbed the ridges by edging upward in a zigzag path. They struggled for footing on the ice-covered rocks as they clutched at bushes and branches for support with one hand while pulling their horses after them with the other. Panting and gasping for breath in the cold air, at last they would gain a summit only to catch glimpses of more wooded mountain ridges ahead and behind, to the right and left. Their progress was torture. The mountains fought them for every step west they took. Christopher Gist somehow followed the nonexistent trail by signs only he recognized.

George knew by now he was not going to be back in Williamsburg in the month Governor Dinwiddie had estimated. How little they knew of the wilderness, the Governor and the Council.

Suddenly, George sniffed the air deeply. "Do I smell smoke?"

Christopher Gist took a deep breath. "You're right, Major. We must be closer to Trader Frazier's than I thought. Come on, everyone. Frazier's must be just ahead. I have not been to his new cabin since he came to Turtle Creek last summer."

George hoped Gist was right. The mere thought of a dry cabin and a hot fire warmed the near ice in his veins. It had the same effect on everyone. They made their horses step a little livelier.

Soon George saw a tiny cabin set close to where a creek flowed into a great river, the Monongahela. There was water on two sides and the trees had been cut back to make a clearing so the forest people who always attacked from cover could not approach too closely. The cabin was obviously newly built, as was the blacksmith's lean-to beside it. The logs were raw from the ax. George was disappointed at the small size of the cabin. He wondered how they would all fit inside.

He urged his horse forward toward the clearing, but Gist grabbed the bridle to hold him back. "Mr. Gist!" George said, his temper rising again at this abrupt act.

Gist did not bother to answer. He fired his gun once into the air and waited a long minute. He cupped his hands around his mouth and shouted, "Frazier? Are you there?" He waited, then repeated, "Hello, Frazier."

George saw the barrel of a gun poke out through a slit in the logs. "Who be you?" a voice came from within the cabin.

"It's Gist, Frazier. Can I ride in?"

"Come ahead," answered a gravelly voice.

"Wait here in the trees until I signal you," Gist ordered.

Barnaby Currin had come up on the other side of George. "Want me t' go in, Mr. Gist?" he volunteered.

"No. I recognize Frazier's voice, all right. But he may not be alone. He may be a prisoner or he may think I am a hostage masking an attack. It has happened before." Gist sighed. "Just see everybody stays back until I signal." A meaningful look passed between Gist and Barnaby Currin, but George caught it. He knew Barnaby Currin would grab his bridle and probably unhorse him if he made a move.

Gist walked his horse forward slowly, holding his gun up but not in firing position. Back in the cover of the trees, Currin and the other traders had their muskets aimed at the cabin. George did not even try to get to his gun. Currin might not understand his move. He felt he was watching some sort of ceremony with elaborate rules that these men knew and had performed many times.

Slowly, Gist crossed the open space before the cabin. The musket poking out the slit was trained on him. The unseen voice said, "You alone?"

"No, I have six men with me," George heard Gist answer.

"Must be real trouble with the French for

Frazier to act this way," Barnaby whispered through his teeth.

Gist turned and waved toward them.

"All right, Major," Barnaby ordered, "Ye 'n I ere goin' in. Jenkins, ye follow with Dutch. Then MacQuire, then Steward. Slow now. Ready, Major?"

George nodded. He was not about to argue command with Currin. He did as he was told. Barnaby raised his gun as Gist had done and they went forward, walking their horses.

When everyone had reined up beside Gist, the door opened and George saw John Frazier, the object of Dinwiddie's concern. He was a great bronze man almost as large as Christopher Gist and himself. He was dressed in half cloth, half animal skin clothes that most frontiersmen seemed to prefer. "Sorry, Christopher," he said.

"Trouble, John?" asked Gist.

"Yes, sir!" Frazier answered tersely. "But welcome all. Get the horses taken care of. Keep 'em close to the cabin. Don't let 'em loose to forage or tie 'em to trees in the woods. I'll get the fire up and put some viands on. Come right on inside and warm yourselves."

George was amazed. This man who two minutes ago was ready to send them all into eternity was now the most freehearted of hosts.

When they entered the cabin, John Frazier bustled about seeing to their comfort. There were no chairs, only log stumps that had been sawed and dragged inside, and there were not even eight of those. The floor was hard-packed earth. But George did not care. He was out of the cold and rain. He edged over to the fire, dreaming about how he would sleep dry tonight for the first time in a week. Frazier stirred up the fire until it was roaring. Gist offered some small game he had shot during the day. It was put on the spit to roast. Potatoes were thrown in the coals to bake. Frazier filled the kettle with water from the creek just outside his door, hung it on the crane, and swung it over the fire. From covered wooden boxes on a shelf, he took dried apples, mixed them with water, and put them on a spider pan over the embers. It all smelled like a feast to George after weeks of fried corn-meal mush and salt pork.

Only after everyone was inside and divested of their wet outer clothing did Gist try to introduce George to John Frazier. "John, may I present Major George Washington, leader of this expedition," he said with great formality as if they were all in Williamsburg. He punched out the words "George" and "leader."

Frazier looked at George and put out his hand. "Pleased I am to see you." But he also gave a questioning look toward Gist.

"The Major is one of the Washington brothers," Gist said meaningfully. "And he has been sent here by Governor Dinwiddie . . . But I will allow the Major to tell you of his mission."

"Part of my instructions from Governor Dinwiddie, Mr. Frazier, is to find out about you," George began. "The Governor is very concerned about you and the fact you . . ." George tried to think of a way to put it politely, "Left Venango last summer."

Frazier smiled wearily. "So Governor Dinwiddie is concerned over me. Aye, 'tis a long story, Major. I have messages for Governor Dinwiddie, too." John Frazier went over to a peg in the logs and pulled off a wide belt made of small black beads strung together on fine leather thongs. Attached to one end was a tomahawk. John threw the belt of beads onto the sawbuck table in front of George and Gist. "Tanacharison left this."

George barely glanced at it. He had been advised in Winchester to buy wampum as gifts to the tribes because they seemed to value greatly the beads made from clam shells. Strings of it were in his baggage.

But Gist picked up the wampum from the table and examined it carefully. John Frazier explained, "Half King says the Chippewas and the Ottawas have sided with the French and taken up the hatchet against the English."

Barnaby Currin whistled through his teeth. "I don't like that. No wonder ye been careful, John."

"Yet Tanacharison still wants to ally himself with the English?" Gist asked.

"Aye. I guess that's what he means. He left that particular wampum as a message to Governor Dinwiddie that he's siding with the English."

"Yes, the black wampum and a hatchet. An invitation to the Governor to make war against a common enemy," Gist said, as he continued to hold the string of black shell beads in his hand.

George interrupted. "Tanacharison. That is the name Governor Dinwiddie told me to contact. Tanacharison is an important man of the Six Nations."

"He represents the Seneca nation," Gist told him.

"But what is he doing around here? The Senecas and the Mohawks and the Oneidas and the other tribes of the Six Nations live east of Ontario Lake or so I have been told?" asked George.

"The council of the Iroquois sent him and other leaders here to oversee the Delawares, Shannoahs (Shawnees), and other tribes they have subjugated in the Ohio country," Gist explained.

"You mean the Indians have that much of a formal, organized government that they appoint men to act as governors?" George was skeptical.

"I suggest that you give these people and their government respect from now on, Major Washington, if you hope to deal with them." Gist spoke sharply. "Long ago, the Iroquois formed themselves into a confederacy of six powerful tribes. They can field a thousand braves in a single war party. Those braves can travel a thousand miles on foot or horseback in a matter of days, living off the land or going without food or water completely for as long as necessary. They have either destroyed or conquered almost every Algonquian tribe east and west of the mountains. They have killed off nearly every Huron in existence. When I lived in Baltimore, I once read the writings of a Jesuit missionary who said about the Iroquois a hundred years ago, 'They approach like foxes, fight like lions, and fly away like birds.'"

"That about describes 'em," agreed Frazier.

"Bloodthirsty devils," exclaimed George, repeating the expression he had heard all of his life spoken with the word Indian.

"Oh no," Gist corrected him. "The Iroquois do not make war for glory. The Iroquois make war because they have been trading with the Europeans since the Dutch came to the New World. They have become accustomed to what the Europeans have. A metal knife is so much better than a flint one. A hatchet is sharper than a stone tomahawk. A metal kettle is stronger than a clay pot. A gun is more deadly than a bow and arrow. When the Iroquois tribes had hunted out their own lands for furs to trade to the white man, they started acting as middlemen by getting furs from tribes farther west. The Hurons were afraid of them and refused to trade, so the Iroquois destroyed them. They were in their way. Are they so different than we are?"

George shook his head. "These traders seem to think more and more like Indians the longer they live out here in the deep woods," he thought. "If you consider this Half King, or Tanacharison, and his people your friends, then, Mr. Frazier, the Governor wants to know why you left Venango?" George asked.

"Because the French drove me out!"

"Did not your Indian friends defend you?" asked George.

"They warned me the French were comin' with eight brass cannons. And I sent word to other traders farther out they was comin' so we'd have time to get away or I'd be sittin' in a gaol in Quebec right now," answered Frazier. "But the Indians are not going to get themselves mixed up in white men's quarrels if they can help it."

"Well, Governor Dinwiddie's letter which I carry ought to convince the French of the error of their thinking that this land belongs to King Louis," George said positively. "Then you can return to Venango, Mr. Frazier."

"Don't count on it. Tanacharison told me Governor Duquesne sent a thousand men to build another fort at French Creek twenty miles inland from Fort Presque Isle on Lake Erie. Call it Fort Le Boeuf."

"No!" exclaimed Gist.

"Are the French there now, Mr. Frazier?" George asked.

"Tanacharison said their general, de Marin, died sudden so most of the French have withdrawn to winter quarters till they get a new commander."

"De Marin is dead?" Gist asked unbelievingly.

"Oh no." George felt overwhelmed. He had spent most of the money and traveled for three miserable weeks for nothing. There was no one to give the Governor's letter to. A new commander might not be appointed for weeks and might not arrive in this godforsaken wilderness for months. But he kept thinking about what Frazier had told him and there was something good in it. "If the French have withdrawn north to winter quarters, maybe all the way to Montreal, that could give Virginia time to build forts," he said.

"At least one fort at the forks of the Ohio," Gist said, seeing George's point. "I doubt they go to Montreal. More likely they have withdrawn to Fort Presque Isle or maybe to their fort at the Falls." (Niagara Falls)

"This means we will have to travel farther to find someone in authority to give the Governor's letter to now that de Marin is dead," Gist moaned.

George looked at him in surprise. Gist seemed to have no thought of giving up the mission. "That will take us many more days. And who will that person be?"

"Tanacharison will know more by the time we get to Logstown. He will tell us where we can find the next in command. Just hope that person is not at the Falls."

George asked, "Mr. Frazier, do you truly believe the Iroquois are still friendly with the English and can be kept as friends? They appear to be the strongest and most feared of all the tribes. We need them."

"Aye. The Iroquois have always been more friendly to the English than to the French. The English traders give them better trading goods for fewer furs than the sharp trading French. The French bet on the wrong Indian nation when they sided a hundred and fifty years ago with the Algonquians. Now they are trying to cozy up to the Iroquois. But when Tanacharison was here, he was very angry with the French. They have insulted him again."

"Again? What did they do?" George wanted to know so he would not make the same mistake if and when he ever met this Tanacharison.

"He didn't tell me," Frazier answered.

"You said again. What did they do the first time?" George wanted to find out as much as he could.

Frazier looked at Christopher Gist.

Gist nodded his head. "Tell him, John."

"Tanacharison's father was an old, very respected chief. Tanacharison claims the French and their Indians tortured the old man to death. Then they boiled and ate him."

Chapter Four

The Indians

Saturday, November 24, 1753—Logstown on the River Ohio

Half a day's journey downriver from John Frazier's cabin, the still, deep Monongahela River flowing from the southeast and the wild Allegheny River flowing from the northeast met at right angles. They swirled together around a triangle of land to form the highway of the wilderness—the River Ohio. Eighteen miles beyond this place called the Forks of the Ohio, Washington saw the wigwams, cabins, and bark houses that made up Logstown scattered on a stretch of low land close to the river.

It was after sunset but not quite dark as the Englishmen rode into the village. The shadows were already black behind the longhouses and wigwams. From the center of each dwelling, trails of thin smoke curled up. A few dogs came out to yap at them. There was no other greeting either friendly or hostile, only the silent stares of women and children as they peered out from their robes of fur.

Christopher Gist led the party through the town until he stopped in front of a large log building clearly constructed by a trader.

"What's this?" George asked curiously as he looked at the structure so out of place in this town of native people.

"A storehouse. Belongs to Croghan. He lives here when he is in Logstown. But he allows other English traders to use it."

"Croghan again. Why didn't Dinwiddie send the great Croghan on this mission?" George mumbled to himself. For once his mind worked quickly. No matter how well the people thought of Croghan, he must not be identified with anyone other than the English King. Before anyone could dismount, he said, "I think not for me, Mr. Gist. We have a stout tent. Just show me a good place to pitch it."

The traders groaned. Jacob Van Braam eyed the relative safety of the storehouse. Gist was almost speechless. "Major, why stay in a wet tent and freeze when we can be comfortable in this building?"

George stubbornly refused to explain himself. "Mr. Gist, I will use the tent. Where can we make camp so we will not interfere with the activities of the people here? We must get on with the business of this expedition. I intend to call upon Tanacharison as soon as possible, indeed, this very night."

"Very well, Major!" Gist said through clenched teeth. He led the party of horsemen to a meadow outside the town.

"Raise the tent and unpack. Tether the horses. Do not let them run loose with just the bells tonight," George ordered, while still mounted on his horse. "And now, Mr. Gist, we shall call upon Tanacharison. What do I do when you introduce me to him?"

"Hold up your hands, palms open, to show you hold no weapons. And do not call these people Indians, at least not where they can hear you. That is an English word, not theirs. Each tribe considers itself an independent nation with its own language, laws, customs, and land. Tanacharison, who we call Half King, is an important member of the Seneca tribe called the Nundawao, people of the great hill. He is also a diplomat of the Six Nations, or League of the Iroquois, as the French call them. The Six Nations is the Hodenosaunee, which means people of the longhouse. Use these names when within their hearing. I have always suspected these people, especially the leaders, understand more English and French than they care to have us know."

George nodded his head. "I will do my best to remember." In his mind, he pronounced the difficult words over several times to commit them to memory.

Excited now that the time was at hand when he would soon meet Tanacharison, the great leader of the forest people, he asked Gist, "Will you explain to Tanacharison why we have come to Logstown?"

"I speak very little Indian languages," Gist admitted.

George exploded. "A fine time to tell me, Mr. Gist, as I am about to meet Tanacharison. I was counting upon you to be my interpreter. Why did you not say something sooner?"

"Major Washington, I was a merchant in Baltimore until a few years ago when I migrated to the Yadkin River in the Carolina colony."

"But you have traveled through the wilderness. You boasted to me you lived two winters with the Indians."

"I did not mean to boast or mislead you. But it takes many years to learn the complicated dialects. And, as I said, every tribe speaks a different language," Gist explained, trying to calm the young major.

"Then just how did you manage in the wilderness?" George asked cuttingly.

"I used sign language, depended on English traders I met, and some Indians know a little English."

"What about Currin or MacQuire?" George was desperate.

"There are many traders holed up here at Logstown. We will find somebody who speaks the Hodenosaunee dialects."

George's anger was so great, he dared not speak. If he continued to quarrel with Gist, he might leave the expedition. George had to consider the great importance of his overall cause. This mission was too vital to Virginia, to all the colonies, to let personal differences scuttle it. He clamped down his iron self-control. At last he said, "Then shall we be about the business of finding a suitable interpreter, Mr. Gist?" George wheeled his horse around to go back toward the town. But he could have waited, for a party of Englishmen was coming toward them.

When Gist, Currin, and the other traders saw the men approaching, they let out whoops and hollers and went to meet them. With much backslapping and carrying on, the traders greeted each other.

George, still mounted on his horse, watched. He made no attempt to join in, for he sensed he would not be welcome. From meeting Gist and Frazier as well as other traders over the years and listening to their talk, he had learned that the long traders were a fraternity of shadowy men.

Men like Gist, Croghan, Trent, and Frazier were major traders who dealt directly with merchants in the British ports along the Atlantic coast. From the merchants they obtained cloth, knives, mirrors, wire, needles, thread, buttons, and jewelry to trade to the Indians for furs. The major traders then transported the furs back to the merchants who sent them to England. Gist and the other major traders were too few to travel through the vast lands beyond the Allegheny

Mountains, so they got furs from other traders who, for many reasons, did not want to go to the British settlements. Some of these traders were known to be indentured servants who had escaped from their contracts for years of servitude in exchange for their passage paid to the New World from Europe. A few were escaped convicts sent to the colonies by the courts in Mother England to serve out their sentences despite the protests of the honest settlers. Whether the traders were big or small, gentlemen or criminals did not seem to matter. Their courage to enter the wilderness, remove themselves for years from their fellow countrymen, and deal with the Indians on *their* terms resulted in mutual admiration. Traders subjected themselves to fearsome tests of loneliness, incredible dangers, and total reliance upon themselves. The survivors were set apart from other men.

As he watched, George saw Gist leave the gathering and bring another man with him. The fellow wore an animal skin for a hat.

"Major Washington, may I present to you Mr. John Davison, whom I can vouch for as an interpreter especially knowledgeable in the language of the tribes here and to the north. John, this is Major Washington of the Virginia militia and the leader of this expedition."

John Davison opened his mouth in a toothless grin. "How do you do, Major?" He did not remove his hat.

George remained astride his horse, looking down on the trader. "Mr. Davison," he answered coldly.

Christopher Gist broke in. "John operates a trading business here in Logstown."

George ignored him and continued to study Davison.

"John has been employed by the governors of the Pennsylvania colony during negotiations with the Hodenosaunees. He has acted as interpreter for Tanacharison for years," Gist added.

"Mr. Davison," George began, his tone somewhat less cold. "I have need of an interpreter here and up north for possibly a few weeks. Would you be available to join my expedition? You would be compensated, of course, in silver."

Davison's eyes lit up at the mention of real money just as Currin's and the others' had. Money was so scarce in the colonies that tobacco had become the medium of exchange east of the mountains and barter in the wilderness. "I am the man to help you for as long as you want me," he grinned broadly.

George was taken aback. Davison's scruffy appearance was the opposite of his proper English speech. "Very well. Then we can begin at once. I intend to call upon Tanacharison. You shall go with me now."

"He's not here," John Davison announced.

"Where is he?" George asked impatiently.

"Out to his hunting cabin about fifteen miles from here."

"I see," George said, as he shook his head. No matter where he turned, walls rose up to block his way.

"Monacatoocha is here, Major," Gist put in.

"Who is he?" George asked disinterestedly.

"He is an Oneida chief sent by the council of the Iroquois to oversee the Shannoah (Shawnee) people here in Logstown. Teach them the Hodenosaunee language and laws. He is considered second only to Tanacharison."

"Then we shall call upon him."

"I suggest we go on foot, Major. It is considered a courtesy," Gist said.

"Very well." George dismounted.

"And a small gift would be a good thing," Gist added. "Wampum to show good faith and perhaps some tobacco to show you have come in peace."

George went to the horses, pulled off some packs, and dug around for a few minutes until he came up with wampum and tobacco. Finally, the three men started toward the longhouses.

For the first time since arriving in Logstown, George saw native men. Two came out of the largest longhouse as the Englishmen approached. They were very tall, as tall as George and Gist. They stood ramrod straight and squinted at the callers with black eyes. Their heads were bald except for a ruff of hair that stood straight up in the middle of their scalps from their foreheads to the backs of their skulls. They wore soft moccasins tied around their ankles and leather leggings topped with loin-cloths and a short kilt. Shapeless doeskin shirts hung from their shoulders.

Everyone waited for George, but he did not know what to say. "Please, Mr. Gist, how do we begin?"

"John, tell these guards we seek a meeting with the great chief Monacatoocha. We have a message from his great English brother."

When Davison had repeated this in tribal language, one of them silently disappeared inside the longhouse. As the Englishmen waited, George tried to control his nervousness by studying the structure. Longhouses were made of tree branches tied together and covered with elm bark. They were about sixty feet long, eighteen feet or so wide, and maybe fifteen feet high. He nudged Gist. "What is that carved wooden totem of an animal hanging above the entrance?"

"It shows the clan to which the family occupying this longhouse belongs."

Soon a middle-aged man appeared in the doorway. He squinted in the darkness at the Englishmen. "Annosanah! Annosanah!" he cried.

"Great chief Monacatoocha. How pleased I am to behold you in good health," Gist said, and Davison translated.

"It has been two winters and two summers since Annosanah has been in my lodge. Too long. Too long." He gestured for them to enter the longhouse.

George followed Gist and Monacatoocha down a corridor about five feet wide. Off this hallway were rooms where he noticed men, women, and children. He was careful not to stare, but he could not resist stealing looks out of the corner of his eye.

They came to a large open area in the center of the longhouse where a small fire burned in the center. Over the fire was a metal kettle suspended from crossed sticks. The ground was packed hard and spread with buffalo robes. Animal skins, rattles, feathers, lances, and grotesque masks carved out of wood decorated the walls. Here and there, hung among the trappings of the Indian family, were the scalps of their enemies. George shuddered.

The chief said a few words to an old woman. She looked at the visitors carefully.

Davison said, "She is the chief woman of the longhouse. It belongs to her and Monacatoocha must ask her if we are welcome. She bids us sit on the buffalo robes now."

Gist smiled and bowed to the woman. George followed his example. She nodded solemnly in return.

When they were seated, the woman took a ladle made of what appeared to be an animal horn and began spooning stew out of the kettle into pottery bowls. She gave one to each of the guests and the chief.

George was very hungry, but when he looked at the contents of the bowl, he suddenly lost his appetite. He recognized pieces of corn and pumpkin, and something that looked like a cousin to the onion floating in the thick grease. An open eye of a fish still attached to a piece of its head stared up at him.

"Eat it! All of it!" Gist hissed. "Not to offer food or be invited to sit on a buffalo robe is an insult to a guest. Not to eat what is offered is a bigger insult to the host!" Gist plunged his fingers into the bowl and ate nosily, smacking his lips and nodding his head.

The head woman of the longhouse smiled.

George summoned all his self-control as he forced himself to stare back at the fish's eye. Silently, he commanded himself, "I will not vomit!" But as he gagged on the fish eye, he thought that he would rather starve.

After all had partaken of the food, Gist said through Davison, "Great chief, this is Major George Washington, sent from the Governor of Virginia—Dinwiddie." Gist nudged George. "Tell Davison what you want the chief to know," he whispered.

George cleared his throat. His eyes smarted from the smokiness of the room. He wanted to slap at the vermin that had begun to crawl on his knee breeches. But he dared not in case such a gesture might be considered an insult. George cleared his throat again. "The Governor sends his greeting to the great chiefs and all their people whom he considers his brothers."

Gist nodded in agreement.

When this apparently pleased Monaca-toocha, George pulled out the wampum and the tobacco. These presents met with the chief's approval, so George went on. "The Governor of Virginia asks that I talk to all the great men and chiefs and deliver his message of friendship to his brothers. Therefore, I would see Tanachar-ison as soon as possible."

The chief answered that he would send a runner to give the message to Tanacharison in the morning at first light.

"Tell Monacatoocha I thank him," George instructed.

"Invite him now to your tent," Gist whispered.

When George frowned and looked puzzled, Gist said urgently, "It is courtesy and expected."

George hesitated, trying to think of the proper words to instruct Davison to use. He cursed his failure to have a quick wit. "Well, what would I say to another Englishman who has just entertained me in his home?" George knew the chief was looking at him expecting him to speak. He could feel the tension building in Gist sit-ting by his side. Finally, he said, "Mr. Davison, will you invite the chief to visit our tent which should be up by now? Tell him it is most humble compared to his fine dwelling here, but we hope he will understand we have had a long journey."

"These people have no word for humble," Davison answered.

"All right, use the word poor. Just get the idea across we want to repay his hospitality."

Davison uttered the clipped low sounds of the Hodenosaunee language to Monacatoocha.

The chief nodded his head solemnly as Davison spoke. Then the tall man gracefully got to his feet in seemingly one catlike movement, picked up a buffalo robe to wrap around himself, and walked back down the corridor and out of the longhouse. He led the party in total darkness through the village until they saw their campfire across the meadow. George hoped Van Braam had made the traders raise the tent instead of going off with their friends to drink and swap stories. Had they had put some food over the fire so he would have something to offer Monacatoocha? He wondered what else he was expected to do to entertain this very important chief. Again he decided to rely on common courtesy.

When they arrived at the tent, George introduced the chief to the other members of the party, invited him inside, and offered him some supper, such as it was. George spent an uncomfortable hour not being able to tell if Monacatoocha was pleased or dissatisfied as he ate. When the chief finished his food, he departed without any words of farewell. George felt he had not made a good first impression on this important leader.

The next morning, George and Gist were sitting in the tent, each making entries in his journal about events of the past few days, when Barnaby Currin burst in. "Gist! Gist! Some Frenchmen just came into town!"

George jumped up. "We're being attacked?"

"No, no," Currin said. "They're soldiers, all right, but they're deserters. Came in with a trader name o' James Brown. Ye know 'im, Gist?"

George did not give Gist a chance to answer. "I've got to question them. They must have much information. Get Mr. Van Braam. Where are they, Mr. Currin?"

"Over t' Croghan's place."

"We must go at once. Where IS Van Braam?"

"Here, Major," said the Dutchman, who had come into the tent to see what all the excitement was about.

"Some Frenchman are here. I will need you to interpret," George told him.

Van Braam was excited to be of some importance at last. "Oui," he said. "Je parle français très bien" (yes, I speak French very well).

George struck out across the meadow toward Croghan's storehouse with his long stride, Van Braam, Gist, Currin, and the rest of the expedition at his heels. When they came to the storehouse, George felt excited; these were the first French soldiers he had ever seen. But he sternly warned himself, "These men are not only Frenchmen, the enemy, they are the worst of the enemy, deserters. They deserve no consideration nor can I believe much of what they may say." He hoped he was contorting his face into a grim expression. But when the four prisoners saw him, he could see they were terrified.

George talked first with Trader Brown. "Where did you find these men, Mr. Brown?"

"Beggin' yer pardon, Sir, they found me. Surrendered to me near lower Shawnee Town. I kin tell ya, Sir, I was might' afraid when I met 'em."

"What were you doing so far from Logstown when the French have been capturing English traders?" George wondered at the man's foolish bravery or sheer stupidity.

"Well, Sir, I work alone down the Ohio tradin' fer furs. I ain't been back here t' Logstown fer some years n' I ain't heard o' all this trouble with the French till but lately. That's why I'm comin' in now—in the middle o' my best season. I'm comin' upriver when I met these Froggies. Said they'd travel with me if I'd point 'em the way t' Philadelphia Town."

"What did these men tell you while you were

traveling together?" asked George.

"Well, Sir, I don't speak no French n' they don't speak no English nor Indian. An' there bein' four o' them n' only one o' me, I didn't ask questions o' them."

George was disappointed. "Yes, of course. Well, I'll just have to ask them directly. Mr. Van Braam, ask these men where they are from."

Jacob Van Braam repeated the question in French, assuming now the tough, threatening manner of a military officer toward captured soldiers.

The Frenchmen seemed to understand his French, which George hoped was better than his English.

"Men say they mean no trouble. Just want to get out of Indian country. Want to go to English settlements," Van Braam said.

"Ask them where they are from again and how many men and guns they had before they deserted," insisted George.

Again Van Braam translated.

The Frenchmen looked at each other. One, evidently the leader, spoke in flowing French speech that did not sound much like Van Braam's.

Nevertheless, Jacob seemed to understand them. "Say they come from New Orleans, up the Mississippi River with one hundred men, eight canoes, provisions. Supposed to meet on River Ohio at Great Beaver Creek with men and canoes come from Lac du Chat (Lake Erie). But soldiers from north not come. Men scared. Decide to run away."

"If they had met the soldiers from the north, then what were they to do?" George asked.

"Think they go north up River Ohio," Van Braam translated.

To George, this information was worse than Governor Dinwiddie had even suspected. The French were bringing reinforcements from New Orleans. They had discovered a water route between New Orleans and their settlements in Canada. Dinwiddie thought all their forces to take over the lands of the Ohio country would have to come from Montreal or Quebec.

"Ask them how far New Orleans is from here and how many men and cannons they have at New Orleans."

"Thirty-five companies forty men each. Strong fort with carriage guns," translated Van Braam.

"Almost fifteen hundred soldiers. Not militia either, but regular, trained soldiers as these men are. The danger grows larger. How many forts on the Mississippi?" George asked.

"These men say four small forts between New Orleans and the country of the Illinois," Jacob said.

"Illinois?" George repeated. "Mr. Gist, do you know of Illinois?"

Gist shrugged his shoulders and shook his head.

"Ask them again, Mr. Van Braam, and tell them I want the truth this time," George said, trying to look tough.

"Où est Illinois?" (where is Illinois?) asked Jacob.

The Frenchmen replied, waving their hands as they tried to make themselves understood.

"Say fort at Kaskaskia. Has one hundred twenty men, six cannons. It thirty leagues above mouth of River Ohio, which is one hundred fifty leagues above New Orleans. I think they mean Isle Noires—Black Islands, Major," Van Braam said, trying to be helpful.

"Black Islands?" repeated George, looking at Christopher Gist.

"Never heard of them."

"Ask them how many men are at the forts on the Mississippi."

"Thirty, forty men, some small cannons each," Jacob translated.

"What other forts do the French have?" George asked.

Van Braam relayed the question, then the reply. "One small fort at mouth of Obaish (Wabash) River. It heads at west end of Lac du Chat. Flows to Ohio sixty leagues from Mississippi. This how French on Mississippi send messages back, forth to Montreal, Quebec."

Again George turned to Gist. "Where is the Obaish River?"

"I do not know," said Gist.

George paced back and forth. He wished he knew how far the Mississippi River was from here now he knew the Ohio flowed into it. And if this Obaish River connected Lake Erie to the Ohio and the Ohio to the Mississippi and then to New Orleans, the French could go anywhere they wanted to go. And with forts built and men already manning them, they possessed the continent, a continent the English knew virtually nothing about.

"Heaven help us!" George cried. "We will have to raise men and arms, send at once to London for regular troops, or we will be pushed into the sea by the French."

Chapter Five

The Calumet

Sunday, November 25, 1753—Logstown, Valley of the Ohio

About the middle of the afternoon, John MacQuire ran to Croghan's storehouse. "Major! Major!" he burst in, "Half King is here!"

"He came! Monacatoocha did send for him!" exclaimed George.

Gist looked at him strangely. "Did you think he would not?"

"Well, you do not know about the word of an Indian," George answered carelessly.

"You have much to learn about the honor of the Hodenosaunees, Major," Gist said.

"Where is this Tanacharison, Mr. MacQuire?" George asked.

"He's at his cabin. He don't live in no longhouse."

George nodded. "Mr. Gist, shall we go?" But George stopped halfway out the door. He had forgotten about the deserters. "Mr. Currin, stay with these Frenchmen. See they get something to eat, but continue to detain them until you hear from me."

George and Gist started toward Tanacharison's cabin, which was set apart from the longhouses and wigwams. Soon Davison ran up to join them. As they approached Tanacharison's dwelling, George indicated for Gist to go ahead. Gist knocked at the door. It was opened by Tanacharison himself. Gist held up his hands in the sign of peace and friendship. "Aguyase! Great Tanacharison of the Nundawao (Senecas) and chief of chiefs of the Susquehannah, Shannoah (Shawnees), and the Leni-Lenape (Delawares)." Gist listed his titles as if he were the King of England.

George was glad Gist was saying all these things for he would have choked uttering such flattery. It was his nature to be sincere. As Gist spoke, George could see Tanacharison's face and manner assume great pride and pleasure.

"Annosanah! Welcome!" he answered, the one word "welcome" in English.

Gist continued. "May I present to you Major George Washington, one of the chiefs of the Virginia militia, sent as a special messenger by your brother, the Governor of Virginia, Robert Dinwiddie." Davison translated the introduction into the Seneca language.

George swept off his hat and bowed. But, in return, Tanacharison looked down upon him, scowling. He made no word or gesture of reply.

George felt his unfriendliness. "Mr. Davison, tell Tanacharison his brother, Governor Dinwiddie, sends greetings, and I invite him to my tent to consult with him and receive his wisdom."

Tanacharison made no move to accept or decline the invitation. He continued to study George. Unlike the friendly Monacatoocha, he did not invite the three Englishmen into his house. Suddenly, he turned back inside his cabin, only to come out a few moments later wrapped in a great robe of beaver fur. Without another word, Tanacharison led the way toward the tent in the meadow. George, Gist, and Davison could only follow meekly in his footsteps.

As he walked behind this leader of the forest people, George was reminded of the portrait of King George that hung in Dinwiddie's office. Instead of a beaver robe, Tanacharison might have been wearing red velvet and ermine for there was an aristocratic presence about him. He was very tall and straight although he was not young. Certainly he was Christopher Gist's age, if not older. Yet a fire of youth was in his dark eyes as well as the wisdom of his years. When he spoke, his voice was deep, commanding, even though George had only heard him speak two words.

When the four men were settled in the tent, George offered some roast venison which Tanacharison accepted. But George did not offer rum for he felt they must have clear heads. Patiently, he waited while the Seneca finished every morsel of food he was given.

When Tanacharison finally put down his empty tin plate, George began a discussion with him immediately. He did not want a repeat of last night when Monacatoocha ate and then departed. Through Davison, George told Tanacharison that he was seeking the commander of the French. "Can you tell me the way as I am unfamiliar with these lands?"

"De Marin's dead now. The French have made two great houses one day's travel apart. But to travel there would be slow. Too many swamps from the rains. Have to go now by way of Venango. It would take five or six days to reach French great houses." Davison translated Tanacharison's words into English.

George wanted to know about how many miles to the French "great houses" or forts, but he knew the forest people did not think of distance that way, only in reference to time.

Then George took a chance. He instructed Davison, "Ask if he would care to tell me what de Marin had to say to him since he is dead and I cannot ask him myself."

When Davison translated for George, anger came into Tanacharison's eyes, and he launched into a tirade against the French. Davison could hardly keep up with the translation. What Tanacharison said was so revealing, George asked if he would repeat it so he could write it down and give it to Governor Dinwiddie. Instead of being angry, the Seneca seemed flattered that what he had to say was worthy of white man's writing. He began again. "When I went to the great house, Chief de Marin was very stern to me. He told me to declare my business. So I said to him on behalf of my people for their well being is the rule of all my action. I am as a father to my people," Davison said, repeating the Seneca words in English. George thought this a noble sentiment. Too bad English governors, representatives, and kings did not always feel the same protective way.

Tanacharison continued, now warmed to his subject with apparent total recall. "Now, fathers, it is you that are the disturbers in this land, by coming and building your towns, and taking it away unknown to us, and by force.

"Fathers, we kindled a fire a long time ago, at a place called Montreal, where we desired you to stay, and not to come and intrude upon our land. I now desire you may dispatch to that place, for be it known to you, fathers, that this is our land, and not yours.

"Fathers, both you and the English are white, we live in a country between; therefore, the land belongs to neither one nor t'other; but the Great Being above allowed it to be a place of residence for us, so fathers, I desire you to withdraw, as I have done our brothers the English, for I will keep you at arm's length. I lay this down as a trial for both, to see which will have the greatest regard to it, and that side we will stand by and make equal shares with us. Our brothers the English have heard this, and now I come to tell it to you, for I am not afraid to discharge you off this land."

Although he showed no emotion as he wrote furiously, George could not help but be thrilled by what he heard. Certainly Dinwiddie's letter telling the French to get out, too, might just be enough to convince them to go. Surely they would not try to stand against the English AND the Six Nations.

George had to admire Tanacharison. This man was born to the role of diplomat. He knew the French and the English were ancient enemies and would never join up to fight his people. Therefore, one way or the other, the Six Nations would have the backing of one side especially when Tanacharison offered to share with that side equally. Meanwhile, both sides sought to curry favor with him, which meant supplies of goods and, maybe, guns. The Indians wanted to continue their trade with the French or English, but they would not be ruled by them or give up any more land. George could see now what Gist and Frazier had been trying to tell him about the League of the Hodenosaunees.

"Now I tell what chief de Marin tell me." Tanacharison's dark eyes burned like coals. "He said, 'Now my child, I have heard your speech, you spoke first, but it is my time to speak now . . . I am not afraid of flies, or mosquitoes, for

Indians are such as those. I tell you, down that river I will go, and will build upon it, according to my command . . . child, you talk foolish, you say this land belongs to you, but there is not the black of my nails yours. I saw that land sooner than you did, before the Shannoahs and you were at war; Lead [Pierre Joseph, Céleron de Blainville] was the man that went down and took possession of that river. It is my land, and I will have it.'"

As George listened to Davison's interpretation, he was astounded. "Davison, do you have what the chief is saying correct? De Marin called the Indians but flies and mosquitoes and said the land belonged to the French because of a Frenchman who claimed it for France before the Hodenosaunees conquered the Shawnees that lived here?"

"Yes, Sir. Best I can make out."

George shook his head as he wrote the words down. After the first shock passed, he realized the French were no doubt bragging that the Hodenosaunees could not stop them from coming down the River Ohio. They were trying to scare Tanacharison, hoping he would pass such information along to the English. "Well, their plan succeeded," George thought. He now had new evidence the French intended to take over the Ohio Valley and planned a long war with the English. But was de Marin mad to insult the important Iroquois representative in such a way as to practically guarantee he would side with the English? The French must be strong indeed.

Tanacharison took a dried piece of animal skin from his belt and carefully unrolled it before George. "Here are French great houses. One is big, one small."

George looked at the skin with the plan of the forts upon it that Tanacharison had drawn himself. With a blockhouse in each corner and a stockade all around, they indeed looked strong. "As Gist said, there is no law out here but the law of the tomahawk. I must get that large escort Dinwiddie told me to ask for. Surely the French would not try to take me prisoner with a large force behind me. Or with this information, do I need to go farther? Maybe I should return to Dinwiddie and tell him what I know. For if the French take me prisoner, no information would get back to him," George reasoned to himself.

"Chief Tanacharison, your brother, the Governor of Virginia, told me to seek your advice and wisdom, which you have given to me most generously. I thank you. Your brother also knows some French Indians have taken up the hatchet against the English. Therefore, he desires me to request of you an escort of young men to safeguard against those people who would harm us."

Tanacharison looked at George and Gist for some time in silence after Davison had translated George's words into the Seneca language. At last he spoke. "Tomorrow, I will assemble the great men of the many people, and you will tell them of your business here among us."

George turned to Gist, who had been silent through the whole interview. "What does he mean?"

"He means he wants you to talk to all the chiefs of the local tribes at the council fire. They will decide if we are to get an escort. Tanacharison cannot decide such matters totally by himself."

"I must talk to the chiefs? How?" George shrank from the idea. "What would I tell them?"

"That is up to you. Whatever Dinwiddie wants them to know. But tell Tanacharison you will do it. He is waiting," urged Gist.

George looked at Tanacharison. "Tell him, Mr. Davison, I would be greatly honored to be allowed to speak to the great chiefs as he asks," he said humbly.

Tanacharison nodded his head. Then he got up quickly and was about to leave the tent. But he stopped and spoke to Gist. "Annosanah," he began, then he said a few words in Seneca and was gone.

Davison broke into a toothless grin. "Mr. Gist, your son is all right even if he is a friend of the Cherokees."

Gist laughed. "That man knows everything that goes on in these woods."

George was mystified. "How would he know

76

about your son?"

Gist shrugged his shoulders.

George was relieved for the moment, too. He had felt guilty about Gist's son. But now he had this new worry. "What am I going to say to the chiefs tomorrow? How do I approach them?" George now begged the help of Christopher Gist.

"Just tell them the Governor is their brother. He wants them to give you an escort . . . and so on." Gist seemed not at all concerned. "The council of chiefs cannot be any worse than the Council in Williamsburg and you spoke before them, did you not?"

After their supper of cornmeal and a turkey roasted on a spit, the others rolled up in their blankets and went to sleep. But George lay awake thinking of what he would say to the chiefs. He arose, lit a candle, and pulled out his pen, ink, and paper. Afraid to trust his memory tomorrow when he knew he would be unsettled, he began writing his thoughts down. After hours of writing, crossing out, and writing again, at last he had composed the best he could think of on this cold night. Putting the pen away, he rolled up in his blanket and slept.

The next morning, Gist sent MacQuire to watch the activity at the longhouse that was used as a council chamber. Before midmorning, MacQuire reported that the chiefs were entering the longhouse.

"All right, we will approach and wait to be invited in. We must be there or your request will be ignored, and we must not be late or the chiefs will feel insulted," explained Gist. "The people here have a most elaborate code of what we call protocol and courtesies. In fact, it is more complicated, I wager, than is found at the King's court."

George nodded. He folded the piece of paper the speech was written on and put it in his pocket. He and Gist set off with Davison toward the longhouse.

As they waited outside, George felt even worse than he had in the anteroom of the Council chamber in Williamsburg almost a month ago. All around him stood Mingoes and Shannoahs staring silently. He tried to look and act unconcerned, for he had already learned they admired bravery.

When Tanacharison appeared, he greeted them in a solemn manner. Then he motioned for them to follow him into the longhouse.

Once inside, the smell and the smoke were so overpowering, George was almost driven outside again. All the men greased their bodies liberally with animal fat that quickly became rancid. One man alone in the open air could be tolerated, but the smell of many in a warm, smoky enclosure was suffocating.

George noticed this longhouse was different from Monacatoocha's. There was no long corridor with rooms on either side. It was all one big room. In the center was a smoky fire. The only light came from the entryway and an opening in the roof used as a chimney. Around the walls of the longhouse were platforms a foot or two off the ground. Many middle-aged and old men wrapped in blankets and furs squatted, lay, or sat on the platforms or on fur robes spread on the ground. Unlike the men he had seen around the village, the chiefs' faces were painted with ocher and black soot around their eyes. Red streaks from ear to mouth decorated their cheeks.

Tanacharison took his place next to Monacatoocha on a platform. He motioned for George to sit beside him. Gist and Davison sat next to George. Tanacharison rose to his feet and spoke to the other chiefs. It was quite evident everything George had heard about him was true. From the respectful attention paid to him by the others, he was indeed a chief among chiefs.

George saw Monacatoocha hand Tanacharison a large pipe some two or three feet long. The stem appeared to be made of a strong reed or cane and the bowl was a hollowed out white stone. It was elaborately decorated with feathers and beads.

Each chief rose and put leaves in front of Tanacharison. George recognized dogwood and sumac leaves. Then he saw Monacatoocha pull out the tobacco he had given him as a gift and put it on the ground. Ceremoniously, Tanacharison put the leaves in the bowl of the pipe. When he had finished, Monacatoocha pulled a stick from the fire and lit the leaves.

Christopher Gist leaned over and whispered in George's ear, "This is the ceremony of the calumet. They only do this on important occasions. When you are given the pipe, take two puffs only."

"But I never smoke," George protested quietly.

"If you do not smoke the calumet, it is a sign of war!" Gist whispered fiercely. "When you have taken two whiffs, pass it to Monacatoocha. He is next in rank."

Tanacharison took several whiffs to make sure the pipe was well lighted. Then he handed it to George.

Carefully, George took it, bowed to the chief from his sitting position, and put the pipe in his mouth. He was filled with revulsion, but he took the required two puffs and gladly handed it to Monacatoocha as ceremoniously as possible. "How I wish I could spit right now," George thought to himself.

Monacatoocha took two pulls and handed the calumet to Gist, who took the required whiffs and handed it to another chief. And so the peace pipe was passed around the council until every chief and Englishman had partaken. Then it was placed before Tanacharison and allowed to smolder.

Tanacharison stood again and apparently introduced George. All the chiefs looked toward him and waited.

The picture of the moment he entered the Council chamber at Williamsburg flashed through George's mind. Slowly he got to his feet. Davison stood behind him. George turned to look for reassurance to Gist. Gist nodded for him to begin.

Very deliberately he pulled his speech from his pocket. He willed his hands not to shake, his voice to be steady. "Brothers, I have called you together in council by order of your brother, the Governor of Virginia, to acquaint you that I am sent, with all possible dispatch, to visit, and deliver a letter to the French commander, of very great importance to your brothers, the English, and I dare say, to you their friends and allies."

George stopped and waited for Davison to translate what he had just said. But Davison hesitated and George saw him exchange a questioning look with Gist. Gist shrugged his shoulders and Davison began the translation. When he finished, the chiefs looked puzzled and wary. George realized at that moment that what he said was all wrong. It raised questions about the contents of the letter he was not prepared to answer. But he had started now, so he could do nothing but push on. "I was desired, brothers, by your brother, the Governor, to call upon you, the leaders of the nations, to inform you of it, and to ask your advice and assistance to proceed by the nearest and best road to the French. You see, brothers, I have got thus far on my journey.

"His honour likewise desired me to apply to you for some of your young men, to conduct and provide provisions for us on our way, and be a safeguard against those French Indians who have taken up the hatchet against us. I have spoken this particularly to you, brothers, because his honour our Governor treats you as good friends and allies, and holds you in great esteem. To confirm what I have said, I give you this string of wampum."

George handed a string of white wampum signifying peace to Tanacharison. Then, not knowing what else to do, he sat down.

The chiefs looked at George with much doubt. Tanacharison saw this too, and he began to speak to them. Sometimes his voice was pleading, sometimes forceful, even threatening. Tanacharison was a fiery, persuasive speaker. Yet the chiefs shook their heads. When Tanacharison finished speaking, he evidently signaled the meeting was open to general discussion.

George turned to Davison for translation, but Davison only shook his head. "They're talking in some jumble of tongues which I can't make much of."

George wished he knew what was being said especially about him since the chiefs kept glancing toward him. But he did not need to know the language to realize there was much disagreement among them.

Gist leaned over to speak to him. "Major, the Indians rarely make a decision without giving it at least one night of consideration. I would be much surprised if they gave you an answer this morning."

George was impatient. "I cannot delay. If they will not give me an escort, then we shall have to push on alone. Do you know the way?"

"To Venango? Yes. But remember we are closer to the French Indians."

Finally, Tanacharison stood up. There was silence again. He began to speak. "Now, my brothers, in regard to what my brother the Governor has desired of me, I return you this answer.

"I rely upon you as a brother ought to do, as you say we are brothers and one people: we shall put heart in hand and speak to our fathers the French concerning the speech they made to me, and you may depend that we will endeavour to be your guard."

When Davison told him what the chief had said, George was elated. He had succeed in persuading Tanacharison to help him.

But Tanacharison had more to say. "Brother, as you have asked my advice, I hope you will be ruled by it and stay till I can provide a company to go with you. The French speech-belt is not here, I have to go for it to my hunting cabin; likewise, the people which I have ordered in are not yet come, nor cannot till the third night from this, till which time, brother, I must beg you to stay. I intend to send a guard of Mingoes, Shannoahs, and Delawares, that our brothers may see the love and loyalty we bear them."

"Stay! How long?" George asked.

"Three nights," Davison answered.

George did not try to hid the disappointment he felt at Tanacharison's delays over some strings of beads. He stood and made his reply to Tanacharison through Davison. "I thank you, brother, on behalf of myself and your brother, the Governor, for your great concern and desire to help us as he requested. Trust that I will tell him of your great kindness to us. But I have orders from the Governor to make all possible haste with my business and I cannot wait three days."

Anger flashed in the eyes of Tanacharison and his handsome face became very stern as Davison told him what George had said. When the chief gave his reply, George saw Davison look suddenly fearful. "The chief says he can't let us go without the guard his brother wants. Should some accident happen to us, it would reflect on him. He also says this is an important matter and can't happen without much counsel for he now

84

wants to give up the French speech belt and make the Shawnees and Delawares do the same."

"Cannot let us go . . . ?" George started to repeat, then stopped. Panic welled up inside him. He recognized he had placed the goals of his expedition in great danger by not submitting to Tanacharison's plans. He looked to Gist to smooth things over. But Gist stared back silently, his knuckles white as his hands gripped the edge of the platform. It was up to George alone to reduce the danger, if he could.

Weakly, he told Davison to say, "Great chief, I will do as you suggest since you are most wise in these matters."

Tanacharison looked at him suspiciously. George hastened on. "Here, I return the wampum belt you left with Trader Frazier with the message for Governor Dinwiddie that the Chippewas and Ottawas have taken up the hatchet against the English. I would wish you to tell me directly the speech you wish to be delivered to the Governor."

Tanacharison answered sharply. "No. We tell you message only after we meet in full council with the chiefs."

George could think of nothing else to say. He looked helplessly at Gist.

Christopher Gist said, "We thank the great chiefs for hearing us today and giving our request their consideration. We will await your words about the departure to the French. We thank our loyal and loving brothers." Gist bowed. George and Davison did the same. Then Gist motioned for them to leave the longhouse. The council was over—for them.

Outside, George said hopelessly, "Well, I certainly botched that."

"Major, you were fortunate they even heard you. You are young and the Hodenosaunees respect only age—the older, the better. They listened to you because they felt Dinwiddie spoke through you, his age preventing him from coming in person. Since they think youth speaks only foolishness, they will disregard much of what you said. Be glad of that."

George walked dejectedly back to the cold tent.

On the second day after the meeting of the council, Monacatoocha and a chief called Pollatha Wappia appeared at the English tent with some food. George was pleased. "It is as Gist said, if they like you, they share their food," he thought. George thanked them warmly and invited them into the tent. Then he learned the offer of food was but an excuse.

"Why do you go to the French? Are they not your enemy?" Monacatoocha asked through Davison.

George had been expecting the question, but he could not reveal the contents of the letter he carried. Yet he had to tell them something.

"We do not want to be enemies with the French. The English and French have fought many wars across the great water. We do not want war here." George hoped this would at least satisfy them somewhat.

But Monacatoocha looked at him curiously and said, "But French want war with you."

"Oh?" George said coolly.

Monacatoocha went on eagerly as Davison translated. "A runner came two, three days ago from Venango. He said that French Chief Joncaire called all Mingoes and Delawares to that place and said the French wanted to go down the Allegheny River last fall, but the water was getting cold and winter was coming. Chief Joncaire said the French will come downriver in greater numbers next spring. He warned the Mingoes and Delawares to stand aside and not take part in the war with the English. Joncaire said the war with the English would take three years. Though they lost their chief, de Marin, and a few soldiers, they had enough men to make themselves chief of the River Ohio. If English were strong, too, they would divide all the land between them." The chief looked worried.

George had a hard time believing the Frenchman, Joncaire, whoever he was, would tell the Indians so boldly of the French plans. Still, the gossip Monacatoocha told him did make him more anxious to be on his way.

George therefore was not pleased when

Monacatoocha again appeared at his tent early the next morning, this time accompanied by Tanacharison.

"We must stay at this place one more day because the Shannoah chiefs have not brought the wampum in as they were ordered to do. But they will have it here by night. Nor has Chief Shingiss of the Delawares. He says it is with another chief in Venango," John Davison translated.

George saw Tanacharison was sincere. He did not understand the full importance of the wampum belts, but they were of great importance to the Indians. If the returning of the wampum meant the Indians were abolishing agreements with the French, then the delay would be worthwhile. He remembered Governor Dinwiddie's words to win the Indians to the side of the English for they held the balance of power if war came. Without showing the impatience he felt, George said, "Of course we will wait as you think best, Great Brother."

This pleased Tanacharison. George was learning his brand of diplomacy.

That night at Logstown, the chiefs met again in council at their longhouse to decide who should go with the Englishmen. Neither George nor Gist was invited. But the council went on much of the night and George did not know its outcome until the next morning when Tanacharison, two other very old chiefs, and a young brave rode up to his tent in full dress, their faces decorated with soot, ocher, and red berry juice.

George sighed. "There is going to be another delay. Well, what is it this time?"

The chief answered. "The great council decided three great chiefs should deliver a speech and the wampum to the French. This would be better than many braves. The French would be frightened and think we come to make war. We not make war in the winter. Bad. Not enough food for war in winter." Tanacharison went on. "Chief Jeskakake will make a great speech to the French and give them the wampum belts of Shannoah and Delaware people." He indicated the oldest of the chiefs.

George thought the old man looked so frail he could not make the journey. George estimated if the mighty Tanacharison was in his forties or fifties, old Jeskakake must be ninety. Since he was a Cayuga chief, he must have been chosen because he represented another nation of the League of the Hodenosaunee or, more likely, he was the most senior chief available.

"Chief White Thunder is from Hodenosaunee, too," Tanacharison said importantly as he pointed to another man not quite so elderly. "Guyasuta will be our hunter so we will have food." He indicated a young Seneca warrior. "We go now."

But George did not move. "Great chief, we

cannot go to the French without many men as you said so yourself in council three days ago. Without many men, the French might take us prisoner and send us to Canada," he protested.

Tanacharison's eyes glared at George. "The Hodenosaunee are greater warriors than any French," he said arrogantly. "We will go now!"

But George knew Tanacharison alone could not protect him. From his own words, he had learned the French no longer respected or feared the Iroquois. And if the chiefs carried through on their word to break with the French and again ordered them off their lands, the French surely would treat them hostilely.

Yet George dared not argue further. He knew he had angered and insulted Tanacharison. Nor could he turn back and show cowardice. Right now he represented England and the King and the Governor. The Indians must be shown the English were not afraid of the French.

He turned to Gist, Van Braam, and the traders. "Gentlemen, if we go ahead without the large escort, we face capture by the French and . . ." He did not finish the sentence. "Therefore, I do not expect you to accompany me any farther on this expedition. I will pay you now for your services and you can return to your own business. I, of course, must go on to deliver the Governor's letter to the French—if possible."

Christopher Gist was the first one to speak. "I am committed to serve as guide, Major."

"You cannot talk to French without me," said Jacob Van Braam. "But we need not fear French. I knew them well in Europe. They are very polite people. They will honor you as diplomat."

"Thank you both."

Then Barnaby Currin spoke up. "We go where Mr. Gist goes."

George looked into their eyes, and each man returned his gaze steadily. George nodded. "Very well. Strike the tent!" he ordered.

By midmorning the party of twelve set out for Venango and the French. Tanacharison, Jeskakake, and White Thunder led the way along the trail. George, Gist, Van Braam, Davison, and the traders followed. George did not entirely trust Tanacharison. He pulled out his compass to check the direction they were being led. A hand suddenly covered it. George looked up, startled, to see Gist glaring at him.

Hoarsely, Gist whispered, "Do not let the chiefs see your compass. They are suspicious of men who use compasses."

George pocketed his compass quickly. He was totally in their power.

Chapter Six

The French

Tuesday, December 4, 1753—Venango

It was like a slap in the face, the sight of the four blue fleurs-de-lis on the white flag snapping in the cold wind atop John Frazier's log house. It made a fiery anger rise in George. For a long time he had heard about the French taking over King George's lands in the Ohio. Now he was face to face with the reality of it. Like George, Christopher Gist's face was grim as he stared at the French flag. To the five traders this flag represented a loss of their livelihood and the capture or death of their friends.

The whole party was drawn up at the edge of the thick forest surrounding the town of Venango where French Creek flowed into the upper Allegheny River. The old chiefs watched the Englishmen with squinting black eyes. Tanacharison gave no orders, made no move to lead as he had on the roundabout seventy-mile journey from Logstown.

George felt their eyes on him, waiting. He knew the longer he hesitated, the weaker his position would be in their eyes. He gathered his courage. "Mr. Currin, you and Mr. Steward, Mr.

MacQuire, and Mr. Jenkins find a place to set up the camp. Mr. Davison, tell the chiefs that if they go with Mr. Currin, they can soon be in a dry place and have warm food." George did not want the chiefs with him when he faced the French for the first time. "Mr. Gist, Mr. Van Braam, courtesy demands I go immediately to seek the French commander so I may present my credentials to him."

Gist nodded silently in agreement. Jacob Van Braam was the only one who seemed eager to go forward. The party split. While the traders and the Indians moved off, George, Gist, and Van Braam slowly rode toward Frazier's house. They knew their every move was being watched. Stiff and straight as befit military men, George and Jacob sat astride their horses. But George's heart was pounding in his ears.

During the four days of travel from Logstown to Venango, George had rehearsed what he would do and say when he met the French. As he approached the building the flag flew over, George could see John Frazier's house was really a cluster of buildings grouped in such a manner so it could be defended against attack. Yet it could not really be called a fort or even a stockade. As they reached the entrance, three French officers came out. They were dressed in white uniforms. Swords dangled from their sides and pistols were tucked in their wide leather belts. "Soyez le bienvenu à Venango, le commandant et monsieurs (welcome to Venango, commander and gentlemen). Je suis (I am) Captain Philippe Joncaire, Sieur de Chabert. Voilà (this is) Commissary La Force et Lieutenant Jean Reynard."

George stayed astride his horse looking down on the three Frenchmen as long as he dared. Then he dismounted; Van Braam and Gist followed him. Standing face to face now, George took some small satisfaction in noting that the two Englishmen still looked down on the Frenchmen who were rather small.

With a bow not quite as fancy as the Frenchman's, he said, "I am Major George Washington, adjutant of the colony and dominion of Virginia. My companions, Mr. Christopher Gist, my guide, and Mr. Jacob Van Braam, my interpreter."

Captain Joncaire and the other two officers bowed and smiled toward Gist and Van Braam. "Bonsoir (good evening), monsieurs, bonsoir. Commandant Washington, Monsieur Gist, and Monsieur Van Braam, please come inside and warm yourselves. You must be tired and chilled from your long journey." Joncaire bowed and gestured toward the log building. No interpretation from Van Braam was necessary.

"Thank you," George said, and followed Captain Joncaire into the house. In the fading light, George covertly studied this Frenchman whose name he had heard so often in Logstown.

He was not young. He was probably born in the same decade as Gist and Tanacharison. Some said he was a half-breed, the son of a high-ranking French officer and a Seneca woman. Others said he was once a French boy sent out by the government in Montreal to live with the tribes and be adopted by them, thus strengthening French influence with them. Whatever stories were true or not, the Joncaires—father and two sons of whom Philippe was one—were as close to the Iroquois as they allowed any Europeans to get.

Captain Joncaire showed George and his friends into a large, room, comfortable by wilderness standards, where a great fire gave welcome heat. Remembering this was John Frazier's once and comparing it to Frazier's current tiny shack on Turtle Creek, George understood his bitterness. He could see all the work Frazier had put in these buildings. He estimated they must be worth five hundred pounds. How unfair it was that he should lose it. But the Frenchmen acted quite at home as if they had lived here for years instead of since only last summer.

"Please allow me to give you some brandy," offered Joncaire, showing George the date on the bottle for his approval.

"Thank you," George replied stiffly. But he allowed himself only a sip. Much as he wanted to talk about his business with the French now that he was face to face with them, the time was not yet right. Captain Philippe Joncaire had received them with faultless courtesy. Now George must play the game of exchanging meaningless polite talk with him. George thanked Providence for the years of training in these very skills given him by his older brothers, Lawrence and Augustine, and Colonel William Fairfax. Now what they had tried to teach him would be put to a severe test. He was very patient exchanging idle chatter through Jacob Van Braam as the bottle of brandy was repeatedly passed around. Gradually, and in an oh-so-friendly manner, the talk of the French took on a questioning nature. Surely the Englishmen were not passing through the wilderness on the brink of cruel winter to take in the great beauty of the River Ohio.

George felt he should be truthful and show that he was here on diplomatic business. "Mr. Van Braam, tell Captain Joncaire I seek the ranking commander of this territory to deliver a letter from Governor Dinwiddie of the colony and dominion of Virginia on the part of His Majesty, King George the Second. Is he that man?"

Joncaire replied, "I have command of the Ohio and I am chief interpreter of the League of the Iroquois. But there is a general officer at the next fort to whom you should give your letter if you seek the highest authority."

When Van Braam interpreted this statement, George quickly let Joncaire know he could not be fooled. "I heard your general—de

Marin—has, most regrettably, died recently."

"Ah, oui. But a new general has been appointed and is expected at Fort Le Boeuf any day now."

"If this man has to come from Montreal or Quebec, it would take months for him to reach here. In fact, he probably will not come at all until spring," George said. "And I will not be sent on wild-goose chases all over the wilderness in winter. How far is it to Fort Le Boeuf, Captain Joncaire?"

"It is but twelve to fifteen leagues up French Creek." Joncaire swept his arm in a wide gesture toward the north.

George's face took on a look of displeasure at such a long trip, forty or fifty miles more. "Then until the new commander comes, you are the ranking person in the Ohio?"

Captain Joncaire said in French, "Commandant Washington, although I am as one with the Iroquois and help the French government care for their children as a captain in the French army, I also run a trading post and portage at the falls of Lac du Chat (Niagara Falls). That is my primary business. I could not assume such responsibility for my government by receiving and answering a letter from a foreign governor. In fact, you should take the letter to Governor Duquesne himself. Yes, in Montreal. That is the best advice I can offer you." He seemed greatly concerned over these weighty matters.

Then he abruptly changed the subject. "Please, would you and your party do the honor of dining with us this evening?"

George knew he should not press the subject now. He would learn more before deciding whether to go on to Fort Le Boeuf or whether to force Joncaire to accept the letter. For now he said, "Yes, indeed, we would be most delighted to accept your kind invitation." Not to accept would be the ultimate insult. Van Braam passed on his acceptance. But George intended that only himself, Gist, and Van Braam would dine with the Frenchmen. His instincts told him not to include the Indians. It was best Joncaire and Tanacharison not meet.

Joncaire called an aide and began giving orders to prepare a dinner. Several soldiers appeared and spread a white cloth on the rough-hewn sawbuck table and laid tinware and utensils.

Jacob Van Braam leaned over to George and whispered, "See, Major? I told you we had nothing to fear from French. Oh ho, you not seen hospitality until treated to French hospitality." Jacob was already quite aglow with French hospitality from the brandy bottle. This caused George concern. Only through Van Braam could he understand the French. "Mr. Van Braam, for the good of this expedition, I order you to restrain your drinking!" he whispered fiercely.

As the evening progressed, the French officers did enjoy their wine, more and more. Lieutenant Reynard brought out a flute. They sang French songs to entertain their English guests while a cask of wine kept their throats in top singing condition. George seemed to enter into the spirit of the evening, laughing and singing along with them, swinging his glass in rhythm to the music. But although giving the appearance of matching them almost drink for drink and becoming as joyful as the French, George actually drank very little. Much of what was poured into his glass disappeared down the wide cracks in the split log floor. For George had seen men drink before, and he knew it could make them jovial or ugly, but it always loosened their tongues. He wanted to be ready.

When the proper time came, George rose to his feet with a full glass of red wine in his hand. "Monsieurs, I give you the good health and long life of His Most Christian Majesty, King Louis the Fifteenth of France!"

This statement from the English officer appealed to the Frenchmen's national pride. Joncaire then arose unsteadily to return the compliment. "I give you the health and long life of George the Second, King of England, Ireland, and Scotland. But not of the Ohio," he put in devilishly.

This brought a roar of laughter from the French. Jacob quickly interpreted as Joncaire went on. "We intend to take the Ohio and all its tributaries and by God, we will do it! It is ours. Our great explorer, La Salle, discovered it sixty years ago and it is ours, I tell you! We know the English can raise a force of two men to our one. But let them. We French can move fast in our canoes. Up and down the rivers, place to place, and the English will be too slow to stop us!"

Slyly, Joncaire looked at George. "We know the English are sending out settlers. We know. But tell them to go back! Back across the mountains! For I, I, Philippe Thomas Joncaire, will not let one Englishman settle on the Ohio or even on one of its tiniest tributaries!" Then he burst into loud laughter and George laughed with him when Jacob had interpreted his words. But George knew, drunk or not, the Frenchman meant every word.

George jollied Joncaire along. "Ha, ha, you are boasting. Where are your men to stop the English? Surely you would not waste your fine cooks in battle." George smacked his lips and stuffed more food into his mouth.

"Men? We have many men. Before General de Marin died, we had fifteen hundred men this side of Ontario Lake. But half were recalled to winter quarters. The rest garrison our forts. We have many forts."

"I see no forts. Venango has no fort," challenged George, baiting them with seeming good humor.

The Frenchmen's Gallic pride exploded.

"We have seven forts with at least one hundred fifty men each between here and Montreal," bragged Commissary La Force.

George laughed skeptically when he heard this from Van Braam.

"We do," insisted La Force. "You will see Fort Le Boeuf when you go there. Then it is only five leagues from there to the south shore of Lac du Chat, where there is another fort where we keep great stores."

George thought, "That must be Fort Presque Isle."

La Force went on. "Then we have another at the carrying place around the Falls where we keep all our stores sent from Montreal. There are four forts between that one and Montreal. One is near the English fort at Lake Oswego. Sailing ships can go from our fort at the Falls to Montreal in four weeks."

George longed for pen and paper to write all this information down. But he could only commit it to memory to be written down when he reached his tent.

He laughed again, pretending not to believe them. "You do not have so many men or you would not have to toady to the Indians."

When Jacob translated this remark to Joncaire, the Frenchman was uproarious. "Of course we use the stupid Indians. Give them a blanket, a few trinkets, some rum, and they are our slaves. Let them go out and get killed; saves

101

us the trouble."

George thought these were strange sentiments coming from a man who had long lived with Indians and might even be half-Indian himself.

The fine dinner of fish, fowl, and venison interspersed with soup, root vegetables, bread, and dried fruits took many hours to consume. Half the long winter night was gone when George, Gist, and Van Braam made their way back to their tent. John Davison was waiting for them. "The chiefs are gone!"

"Where?" Gist asked.

"They didn't see any reason to tell me, Gist. They just went."

"Back to Logstown?" George asked.

"Probably not, Major. They may have moved in with the Delawares here." Gist tried to quiet George's worst fears.

"When did they go?" George demanded.

"Currin and the other fellows put up the tent and made supper. The chiefs ate with us, then they got on their horses and went. Just faded into the trees."

"Didn't you hear anything they talked about?" George asked.

"They didn't talk."

"We might as well turn in. Nothing we can do until first light," Gist suggested.

But George sat up committing to his journal the information he had learned about the

French forts, men, and routes of supply. His fingers were stiff with the cold, and the single candle flickered in the wind. He had to concentrate for his thoughts were all with the Indians. What were they up to? He never should have wasted those four extra days in Logstown waiting for them. For what? What had been accomplished? They had just disappeared again giving him no support.

In the morning, George sent Davison and Currin to learn where the chiefs were. No sooner had they reported back that they were with the Delawares who lived in and around Venango than Joncaire appeared at George's tent.

"Commandant, I have just learned the great Tanacharison came in with your party. Sacrebleu! Why did you not tell me? The great man should have been at our table last night. I fear he will be offended."

George was surprised and most annoyed at this scolding from Joncaire. He wished he were witty and could come back with some clever answer. Or fast enough to think of some excuse. Instead, George said weakly, if truthfully, "After your statements of dislike for the Indians, I felt they would not be welcome."

"Whatever gave you such ideas? I am in charge of all the Iroquois in the Ohio country and their welfare is dear to my heart as well as my duty." Captain Joncaire dispatched a soldier to seek out Tanacharison and the other chiefs and invite them to headquarters where they would receive presents.

"Now, Commandant Washington, come to my headquarters where we will await Tanacharison," invited Joncaire.

George had no choice but to follow. He certainly would not let Tanacharison be alone with Joncaire.

Little time passed before Tanacharison arrived. Jeskakake and White Thunder accompanied him. Much to George's surprise, Joncaire embraced Tanacharison and the other two chiefs like long-lost relatives. "My brother of the people of the great hill, how good it is to see you, and looking well and strong too!" Joncaire said in the Iroquois tongue, which Davison translated as well as he could. "Why did you not come to see me at once? We have been apart many months."

How different was Joncaire's attitude toward the Indians in their presence than it had been when he talked behind their backs last night. The falseness of the man was incredible, George thought.

"Look what I have for you, mon ami" (my friend). Joncaire went to the other room and brought out a few poor trinkets. George thought Tanacharison would be insulted at such a cheap offering to so great a representative of the council of the Iroquois. But Joncaire also brought bottles of brandy. In the Indian's eyes, these made up for the trifles. Joncaire poured brandy for everyone, giving generous mugs to the chiefs.

George waited for Tanacharison to make the speech to Joncaire as he had to de Marin warning him off the land. But Tanacharison said nothing. And Joncaire, unlike de Marin, did not call the Indians flies and mosquitoes, but embraced them as blood brothers and flattered them.

Again and again Joncaire filled the mugs with brandy and the chiefs drank them dry. George could not believe the capacity of the ancient Jeskakake. Surely the old man would kill himself.

Still no words came from Tanacharison. Soon no words could come from him. George felt deep pain at seeing this magnificent man reduced to a drunken stupor. Until this moment, George did not realize he had come to admire and rely on Tanacharison. In his disappointment and disgust at the spectacle of what the French brandy could do to the chiefs, George forgot to keep his feelings from showing in his face. He looked toward Joncaire, and the French captain looked back at him in triumph. George turned on his heel and walked out of the cabin.

The four Englishmen tramped back to their tent in the rain. Gloomily, George said to Christopher Gist, "I feel we are trapped, Mr. Gist. Trapped by the rain; trapped by the clever Captain Joncaire; trapped by the faithlessness of the chiefs."

"Major, the Indians feel a trap closing in on them, too. They suspect the English may want their land just as much as the French do. De Marin told Tanacharison if the French did not win the war with the English, they would divide the land with them and leave the Indians nothing. How much plainer can their intentions be made? An old Delaware chief once said, 'The French claim the land north of the Ohio, the English claim the land south; now where does the Indians' land lie?'"

George interrupted. "But the Iroquois sold us the lands—two hundred thousand acres around the Forks of the Ohio almost ten years ago with the Treaty of Lancaster. What are they complaining about? This is how the Ohio Company acquired title to the land. Fair and square."

"I know," Gist said. "But they do not understand the Europeans' ways just as we do not understand theirs. Some Indians are afraid and think they will be safe if they mind their own business. Others, like Tanacharison, want to try diplomacy. None are ready to fight for their land for then all trade would stop with the French and English. So they will side with whomever seems the strongest."

"Or is a silky talker?" George said. "We must get the Indians away from here; away from men like Joncaire before he makes Tanacharison forget de Marin's words and his determination to break their treaties with the French. But how?

How?" George sat wearily as the rain pounded the canvas of the tent.

"Are you not trained in swordsmanship, Major, the art of dueling?"

"Of course. Although I consider dueling a most deplorable way of giving or getting satisfaction. It is better not to give offense in the first place," George said.

"There are many kinds of dueling and the weapons are not always swords or pistols," Gist suggested. "But the techniques are the same. Thrust. Parry. Feint. Are they not?"

The late December sun had not risen when George was awakened by someone calling his name. At first it seemed part of the dream he was having. Then he realized someone really was calling to him. He jumped up and opened the flap of the tent. "Tanacharison!"

The Indian started to speak rapidly. He obviously was quite sober.

George gathered his wits and held up his hand. "Just one moment, I will call Mr. Davison."

George quickly went back inside the tent and shook Davison, who was rolled up in his buffalo robe. "Mr. Davison, Tanacharison is here. I need you! Wake up!"

"Huh?" Davison looked up at him, trying to force his eyes to stay open.

"Get up, Mr. Davison." By now, George was shaking Christopher Gist, too. "Tanacharison is here."

Gist was instantly awake. "What? Is he sober? Are he and the other chiefs ready to leave with us today?"

"He is alone and on foot. I have a feeling he is stalling again as he did at Logstown."

In a few minutes all three men were assembled outside the tent listening to what Tanacharison had come to say. He made no apology for his actions of the day before. Instead, he now insisted on doing what he could have done yesterday. Deliver his speech to Captain Joncaire and demand the French leave the lands of the Hodenosaunees.

"He wants us to stay here until he makes his speech and gives back the speech belt," Davison interpreted.

"No!" George said. "Tell him he should give his speech to the commander at Fort Le Boeuf, as I will. Joncaire is as nothing. We can delay no longer. It is getting colder every day. Soon the snow will come even to this low country."

John Davison repeated George's words to Tanacharison. George could see anger come into his eyes. His body stiffened. Davison's interpretation only put into words most of what could be read in his face. "The chief says no. He must stay and give his speech in council with Joncaire and the local Delaware chiefs. Joncaire is in charge of all Hodenosaunee business for the French."

George let out a long sigh. He spoke to Gist

out of the corner of his mouth. "What do you advise? Leave without them today or leave without them in two or three days?"

"Ask Tanacharison how long it will take him to make his speech?" Gist suggested.

When Davison repeated the question to Tanacharison, he snapped a brief answer.

"Part of one day only," Davison repeated.

"Very well," George said wearily. "We will wait part of today, but that is all."

When Davison told this to the chief, he nodded his head and went away.

"What else can I do? Better to be here and see what is happening than be up the trail and not know," George said.

By this time, the traders were standing nearby wondering what was going on. "Mr. Currin and Mr. Steward, in order to save some time, take most of the horses and baggage a little way up French Creek and make camp. I feel we will not leave here until almost nightfall and I do not want to spend another night in this place with the Indians so close to Joncaire and his plentiful casks of spirits."

After seeing Currin and Steward packed and off, George, Gist, Davison, and Van Braam strolled over to the longhouse where the council was to be held. Despite Tanacharison being up and about before sunrise, it was not until midmorning before everyone entered the longhouse and the council began.

Again the calumet was lit and passed around. Then the French, beginning with Joncaire, made long, long speeches of welcome and friendship. George became more and more anxious not only that the precious daylight hours were slipping away, but because he was concerned about the French reaction to Tanacharison's speech, if he ever made it.

Finally, Tanacharison stood to speak. George's eyes never left Joncaire's face. He could tell from Davison's interpretation whispered in his ear that Tanacharison's speech contained the same points he had told de Marin. The French had promised only to trade and not to build forts. Tanacharison came to the climax and ordered the French to quit the land in the Ohio country. He backed his words by returning the treaty belt of wampum with the signs of the four towns on it. But Joncaire remained quite undisturbed.

He spoke to Tanacharison in the Seneca language. "Great representative of the council of the Hodenosaunees, I cannot accept this belt. You give it at Fort Le Boeuf to the great commander. I have no power in such important matters. But you can go to Fort Le Boeuf in spring. Warm yourselves at my fire this winter and we will talk of our misunderstandings. We are your fathers and no father would treat his children unkindly."

Joncaire went on and on—jollying, bribing, pleading—to persuade the Indians to stay in

Venango. From his years of living with them, Joncaire knew all their needs, ambitions, and fears.

As George listened to his words through Davison, the Frenchman's appeals seemed so inviting. He studied their effects on the Indians. They listened quietly to this man who was as one with them, who could speak well in their tongue, nothing of his meaning lost in translation. Yet the chiefs remained silent, unreadable. When he stopped, Tanacharison declared the council ended.

George, Gist, and the interpreters went back to their tent and prepared to leave even though the day was almost ended. "Mr. Davison, go over to the Delaware camp and tell Tanacharison I am waiting for him and the two chiefs so we may depart for Fort Le Boeuf as he promised," George ordered.

But soon Davison was back, and alone. "Tanacharison says he can't leave today. Got some business with Chief Custaloga. Seems Custaloga is the local chief here and he was supposed to give the belt to Joncaire, but he wouldn't do it. Tanacharison had to. Now Tanacharison wants to find out what Custaloga is up to."

George looked at Gist.

"Sounds to me that Custaloga is trying to play both sides. He does not want to anger the French, but he cannot defy the Hodenosaunees," Gist said.

"And it sounds to me like all of them are up to some mischief that will be no good for our cause," George said angrily. "Mr. Davison, go back to the Indians and stay close to them. Try to learn just what they are about."

"Yes, Sir." Davison disappeared into the forest toward the Delaware village.

"Ya want the tent struck, Major?" MacQuire asked.

Dusk was upon them. George did not want to go into the woods at night even if they could follow French Creek to Currin and Steward's camp. "No, Mr. MacQuire, I think we will need the tent another night," George said wearily. "We had better see about some food. I do not think Captain Joncaire will be inviting any of His Britannic Majesty's subjects to supper tonight."

George slept fitfully. He could not help listening for Tanacharison to call at his tent during the night. Surely he would come. But only the sunrise eventually came and still no Tanacharison appeared.

But morning did bring someone else. As George, Gist, Van Braam, and the traders finished a breakfast of tea and hominy cakes, Commissary La Force and three soldiers rode up. Seeing them, George felt a ripple of fear, but he reasoned within himself that surely if Joncaire wanted to capture him, he would have sent more than four men.

La Force was all smiles as he dismounted

and approached Washington. "Bonjour (good day), le Commandant, Monsieurs." He bowed elegantly to the Englishmen. "Captain Joncaire has sent me over to escort you and your party to Fort Le Boeuf."

When Van Braam translated these words, George was first speechless, then furious. Before he could say anything, La Force continued, still smiling broadly. "Captain Joncaire, all of us, are most anxious that you reach Fort Le Boeuf. We will ensure that you, on an official diplomatic mission, pass through our land in complete safety. If something should befall you, sacrebleu . . ." La Force looked heavenward. "The governor, non, the king himself, would have our heads. Our two countries are at peace and we will not allow any incident to disturb our friendly relations."

George forced his right fist, clenched at his side, to open. He would not punch La Force in his smile. He would not. But he wanted to.

Instead, George made himself smile and he told Van Braam to say, "Tell Commissary La Force that I could not take him or his men away from their important duties here. I thank Captain Joncaire, but I could not impose on him. His hospitality and courtesy shown us already are too much. We cannot accept more."

When La Force heard this, he waved his hand as if to scatter away George's objections. "Non, non, you praise us too much for the poor things we have been able to offer you in this remote place. You must accept our escort. Your welfare is our first concern. And since you do not seem to have your Indian escort that you arrived with . . ." La Force's voice trailed off as he looked around the camp.

George was embarrassed, which was just what La Force had intended. "Chief Tanacharison had more business to conduct this morning and we must strike our camp. Then we shall be ready to go," George said with a sureness in his voice he did not feel in his heart.

"Of course," La Force said, smiling all the time.

MacQuire and Jenkins struck the tent and loaded the few remaining pack horses. Still Tanacharison did not come, nor did Davison report. The French soldiers sat around smoking their long clay pipes.

George tried to look very busy as if he was not waiting for the Indians. Finally, he took Christopher Gist aside and said in a desperate whisper, "Joncaire has some device for holding the chiefs this morning. Will you go to their village and find out what is going on? But no matter what it is, bring Tanacharison and the others back ready to travel. We will not be made fools of!"

"Maybe we both should go."

"No. I feel Tanacharison has no respect for me," George blurted out. "And he would look foolish in front of the Delawares if he were to seem to follow a boy." George had no time for pretense now.

"I will see what I can do." Christopher Gist slipped into the trees. But the Frenchmen saw everything. "Where is the monsieur going?" asked La Force, still smiling.

"I believe he has need to relieve himself," George answered carelessly as he walked away, leaving Van Braam to translate as he pleased.

It was past midmorning and approaching noon when Christopher Gist, John Davison, and the four Indians appeared. George was greatly relieved to see they were ready to travel. Quickly, he ordered everyone to mount up. The Frenchmen scrambled for their horses.

"Commissary La Force, if you would lead the way," George said with a bow.

"Oui. Suivez moi" (follow me). La Force was no longer smiling.

George let Van Braam ride up with the Frenchman while he rode close to the Indians with Gist and Davison. He did not want them to talk with the Frenchmen since he had noticed La Force spoke Iroquois languages quite skillfully.

Soon they were deep in the forest and Venango was behind them. George said in a low voice to Gist, "How did you persuade them to come?"

"They were ready to spend the winter here.

Joncaire had promised every tribe in the territory all the food they could want for the entire winter. Guaranteed no one would go hungry. I do not know what else he dangled before them. I told Tanacharison he had promised Dinwiddie to take care of us and it would reflect on him if any harm befell us. He must meet and speak to the new commander. As representative of the Hodenosaunees, he had a duty to do that. By spring, the French would be moving downriver in hundreds of canoes as they said they would. Then it would be too late to talk to the commander and deliver the treaty belts to him. I talked so fast, I cannot even remember all I said."

George smiled in satisfaction. "Touché."

"What?" Gist asked.

"I said touché. You know the fencing term meaning we have scored a point. Thanks to you, Mr. Gist, thanks to you."

Chapter Seven

The Duel

Tuesday, December 11, 1753—Fort Le Boeuf

The gloomy day was almost over when the expedition sighted the lanterns of Fort Le Boeuf across French Creek. The stout wooden gates were closed already in preparation for the wilderness night. Feeble candlelight showed dimly from the windows of the barracks outside the fort's high log walls. Campfires glowed here and there.

George closed his eyes and rubbed his hand across them. He was so cold and wet and weary, yet here was another river to cross. He shook his head as if to make his brain give one more thought. After dealing with Joncaire in Venango and spending four days in the company of La Force, George had learned much about the French. They were mostly show. Very well, he would give them a show.

"Mr. Van Braam!" he ordered. "Ford the stream and announce to the commander that I, an emissary from the King of England, wait upon him."

"Ya, Major." Jacob Van Braam sighed. He guided his horse carefully into the freezing wa-

117

ter of the creek. His mount soon was submerged up to its belly and the water lapped the tops of his boots. George winced as he realized how miserable the man must be.

The remaining fifteen men—English, French, and Indians—waited as they watched Van Braam disappear through the great gate into the fort.

It was totally dark before the gate of the fort opened again and several men with lanterns hurried toward the canoes pulled up on the creek bank. With strong strokes, they paddled toward George and his companions. The first man to step ashore was an officer who greeted La Force. Rapidly, they exchanged words in French until La Force pointed at George.

The officer came toward him smiling broadly. "Bonsoir, Commandant. Soyez le bienvenu à Fort Le Boeuf. I am Captain Picard, second in command. I greet you on behalf of our commandant, Jacques Legardeur, Sieur de Saint Pierre," he proclaimed in French and swept a great bow to George and Christopher Gist.

"I am Major George Washington, adjutant of the colony and dominion of Virginia, here on official business on behalf of His Majesty, King George, and his servant, Governor Robert Dinwiddie."

"I have been authorized to extend to you the protection and hospitality of Fort Le Boeuf. Please, if you would board the canoes, we will conduct you to a place of more comfort," Captain Picard said with much bowing.

George was relieved. This commander, St. Pierre, intended to treat him as a diplomat and not as a spy. "So far, so good," George said to Christopher Gist.

"Right now, I don't care if they put us in the guardhouse so long as the bed is warm and dry," Gist answered.

George had to choke back a laugh, but he agreed with every inch of his cold, wet, aching body.

The entire party crossed French Creek in the canoes while the horses swam behind. As they scrambled out on the bank and were escorted inside the gates, George thought he would be taken to the commander of the fort at once. Instead, a door was thrown open to a simple room with some crude beds, a few stools, a table, and a cold hearth.

George immediately protested. "Captain Picard, I wish to see your commander, Sieur de St. Pierre."

Again, the captain smiled politely. "But Commandant, Sieur de St. Pierre has retired for the night. I could not wake him. Mon Dieu, he would be most angry. I will try to arrange a meeting in the morning."

"He retires at six in the evening?" George asked as sarcastically as he dared.

Captain Picard let the remark pass. "We will

have the fires lighted and a supper here in just a short while. We were not expecting so important a guest."

George looked at him and thought, "Liar. Joncaire probably had his Indian expresses up here two days ago." But aloud he said, "You are too kind, Captain Picard," and made a small bow.

"If you would excuse me, Sir, I will go and look after the others in your party. If you wish anything during the night, a guard will be outside your door." With that, Captain Picard bowed himself out.

When Van Braam interpreted, George felt an alarm go off inside him. "A guard, Mr. Gist? For diplomats?"

Much to George's surprise, the night passed uneventfully despite the uneasiness he felt at actually being inside a French fort. He tried to sleep lightly, even thinking of sleeping in shifts with Gist and Van Braam so they would not be taken by surprise. But the fire, warm food, and wine caused the three men to fall into a sound slumber.

In the morning, George was glad he had slept well for he needed all his wits about him. He dressed carefully, putting on the fresh clothes he had brought just for this meeting. Gist, and especially Van Braam, did the best they could with what clothes they had.

When all had made themselves as presentable as possible, George pulled out his large pocket watch. "Gentlemen, it is almost nine o'clock. I think a French gentleman who retires at six in the evening should have plenty of rest by now, don't you? Shall we go?"

The guard outside sprang to attention and almost, but not quite, blocked their way. George ordered quickly, "Mr. Van Braam, ask the guard where the headquarters is."

The guard had no choice but to escort them.

The men crossed the muddy parade ground in the center of the fort. French soldiers performed their duties, some Indians were about, and traders conducted business. George saw nothing of his traders, Tanacharison, or the other chiefs.

At the door of the headquarters, Captain Picard greeted them again. "Ah, Commandant, bonjour. I trust you slept well?"

"Your hospitality was most pleasing after our long, difficult journey," George replied. "And your guard saw to it we were not disturbed," he added pointedly. "But now I wish to present my credentials to your commander."

"Ah, oui, oui. I have informed Sieur de St. Pierre of your arrival. He is waiting." With that, the captain rapped at a rough plank door and opened it. "Sieur Legardeur de Saint Pierre, may I present Commandant George Washington, adjutant of Virginia, Monsieur Gist, and Monsieur Van Braam." He bowed to George and gestured for him to enter.

An elderly gentleman in the white uniform of the French army rose from his chair behind a desk. He was fully thirty years George's senior. Yet he stood ramrod straight and stared at them with one eye, apparently having lost the other one in a long ago battle.

"Soyez le bienvenu, Commandant Washington, à Fort Le Boeuf." St. Pierre bowed.

George was not about to be outdone in manners. He returned the bow. "Sieur de St. Pierre, we thank you for your fine greeting. You may be sure it will be reported to my government." Then he pulled from his pocket the sealed documents he had carried so far. "Sir, I would, by your leave, present to you now for your inspection my passport and commission and a letter to you from Governor Robert Dinwiddie of the colony and dominion of Virginia."

When Van Braam had translated George's words to St. Pierre, the old soldier held up his hands and said in French, "I cannot receive these papers at this time. I cannot read or speak a word of English, I regret to say. I will send for Captain de Repentigny from the next fort who is acquainted with English. Then we can give the papers you carry the proper attention. Now I must beg you to excuse me. I have but arrived here from the Shining Mountains seven days ago and I have much to do."

When Van Braam translated, George could

do nothing but withdraw. But something St. Pierre said amazed him, and he could not wait to talk to Gist when they were alone outside. "Mr. Gist, what are the Shining Mountains? I have never heard of such a place."

Gist frowned. "I have heard Indians say that far, far to the west are very high mountains that are always covered with snow. They shine. But I always thought it was one of their legends."

"St. Pierre said he just came from there."

"Must be beyond the Mississippi."

"The Shining Mountains," George repeated. "Could there be such a place? Maybe the French have even found a passage to the Western Sea. I must learn more."

At two o'clock that afternoon, a soldier ran up to George as he, Gist, and Van Braam walked about the fort studying it. "Commandant Washington, Sieur de St. Pierre requests you to come to his headquarters. Captain de Repentigny has arrived," he said in French.

The Englishmen hurried to St. Pierre's office. Again, the old soldier stood and introduced a considerably younger man. "Commandant, permit me to present Captain Louis de Repentigny who until seven days ago commanded this fort and now is in command of Fort Presque Isle on Lac du Chat."

Captain de Repentigny and George exchanged bows. Then George quickly brought out his papers again. "Sieur de St. Pierre, I would present my letters of introduction."

"Oui," sighed St. Pierre, and accepted the papers George handed to him.

For a few moments, St. Pierre and de Repentigny studied the letters. "Commandant Washington, it will be necessary for us to translate these papers into the French language. Would you excuse us?" The two French officers went into the next room and shut the door. George waited.

For Frenchmen who claimed an almost complete lack of knowledge of English, they finished the translations of the documents in a short time. When they returned to St. Pierre's office, de Repentigny said, "Commandant, I have done my best with these documents. But I feel your interpreter should look at them to correct any errors."

"Thank you," George responded. "Mr. Van Braam, will you study the letter and its translation?"

"Ya, Major." Van Braam took the parchment from de Repentigny and sat down at a table to study it. At length he said, "Captain de Repentigny, bien (good)! I can find no error."

"Very well. Sieur de St. Pierre, I request an early answer to my master's letter as he is most anxious for my return."

"I will call a council of my officers and we will give the utmost study to your Governor's letter. To speed your return, I can offer you several canoes for your use."

George was astonished. "On behalf of my government, I thank you, Sir."

The meeting was over and George bowed himself out the door and into the early December darkness. "They cannot wait to be rid of us, can they, Mr. Gist? I will get an early answer."

After being served breakfast in their quarters, George, Gist, and Van Braam wrapped themselves against the cold and snow and went out to look for Barnaby Currin and the other traders. They found them in somewhat poorer quarters than their own. There was no sign of Tanacharison. George said, "Mr. Currin, we have, I believe, a short time to learn the military strength of this fort. Mr. Gist, Mr. Van Braam, and I will observe the inside. Can you four get outside the walls? I noticed many buildings and canoes as we came in, but it was so dark, I could not see as much as I wanted to."

"No fort can keep Barnaby Currin in if he's not wantin' to stay. I'll get ye the information ye be needing." With that, the four traders slipped out the door and blended in with the other wilderness people around the parade ground of the fort. Soon they passed out the open but guarded gates.

George, Gist, and Van Braam strolled around the fort. The walls were made of heavy logs standing twelve feet tall pounded into the ground at one end and sharpened to a point at the top. Around the walls five feet off the ground were platforms for men to stand on when firing small arms through holes cut in the log walls. At the four corners of the fort were bastions, or two-story square buildings. On the first floor of one was St. Pierre's office. In another was the doctor's lodging. The remaining two were storehouses. George, Van Braam, and Gist climbed into the second floor of one of these storehouses. George stopped and stared. "Will you look at that, Mr. Van Braam. Two cannons capable of firing six-pound balls. How did they get them here?"

"I hear, Major, French build big wagon road from Fort Presque Isle. I think cannons come by ship, and then by wagon here. They do not fit in canoes," observed Jacob Van Braam.

"I think you must be right. They must have two cannons in each bastion, so that is eight six-pound cannons all together."

"I saw a four-pounder mounted before gate when I came across the river other night," offered Van Braam.

George marveled that the French got cannons into the wilderness when he hardly had been able to get through himself.

Portholes were cut in the logs on two sides of the bastion for the cannons to be aimed through. George looked out these portholes to see what was outside the walls of the fort. There were a number of barracks for the soldiers, stables, blacksmith shops, and kitchens. All the construction was new. It all looked like it had been built in a day. George believed John Frazier's statement that Governor Duquesne had sent a thousand men to build it just last summer. "Mr. Van Braam, I must marvel at this fortification. Tanacharison told me this was the smaller of the two forts. What must Presque Isle be like?"

"French have military engineers magnifique—very good," Van Braam said.

"Indeed they do, Mr. Van Braam. I wish we did. Success or defeat will depend on it if war comes."

As they left the bastion, Barnaby Currin called to them. "Major, I got news!"

"Tell me, Mr. Currin. I think we can safely talk here instead of inside where someone could be listening on the other side of a door or wall."

"Me n' Jenkins counted fifty canoes o' birch bark and one hundred seventy o' pine down by the creek. Many more were being blocked out. These ain't just regular canoes, these be coureur de bois canoes. French fur tradin' canoes. They be thirty, forty feet long. Need five or six men to paddle them. They can carry five, six tons o' goods."

"How many men would you estimate man this fort?"

"Seein' the barracks n' forges n' other buildings outside the wall here, I'd say 'least a hun'red, not countin' officers."

"And another hundred or more at Fort Presque Isle just a day's travel away. In addition are those at the forts Joncaire told us about plus those on the way from New Orleans. We must get back to Virginia so the colonies can prepare to repel this takeover of the Ohio."

"How?" Gist asked. "The French have too much of a head start. They have two forts and two or three hundred soldiers here now. We have no forts for hundreds of miles and one soldier—you."

George ignored him. "I must find Tanacharison and see he gets his business taken care of so we can leave in a day or two at the most."

"Major, I seen some o' the French officers with Tanacharison and the others passin' the whiskey jug around," Barnaby related.

George sighed. "Try to find Tanacharison and either let me know where he is or talk him into visiting me."

"Yes, Sir." Currin headed for the gate of the fort.

Early the next morning, Currin, Davison, and Tanacharison appeared at George's quarters. George asked impatiently, "Chief Tanacharison, have you returned the treaty belts to Sieur de St. Pierre and made your speech?"

"St. Pierre cannot talk to me. He is busy. He send us many presents, but he cannot talk,"

Tanacharison said through Davison.

George immediately saw through St. Pierre's delaying tactics. Evidently, he thought differently about Tanacharison than de Marin did. "But you must make your speech and return the belts as you promised. I must leave very soon and I will need the protection of the Hodenosaunee chiefs. Please, ask him again to talk with you."

"I know what I must do," Tanacharison said through Davison. "I need no one to tell me."

George realized he had overstepped his place again. "Of course. I rely on your wisdom," he said humbly, but his fists were clenched in impatience.

Soon after Tanacharison left the room, a soldier knocked. "Commandant, Sieur de St. Pierre invites you to his headquarters," he said in French.

"The answer must be ready, Mr. Gist. Then we can leave."

"None too soon for me."

In a few minutes, they were shown into the presence of St. Pierre, Picard, de Repentigny, and, this time, La Force. St. Pierre cleared his throat. "Commandant Washington, after reviewing this letter from Governor Dinwiddie, I must advise you to take the letter to Governor Duquesne in Quebec. I am but a wilderness commander."

When Van Braam interpreted this statement, George's temper flared. "No! If my master had wanted to address Governor Duquesne, he would have sent a ship to the St. Lawrence River. My orders are to deliver his letter to the commander of the Ohio Valley. I have no authority to go farther or to give the letter to anyone else."

"But Commandant Washington, this is too important for me. Please go to Quebec," St. Pierre pleaded.

"I cannot," George said stubbornly. Quickly he changed the subject and went on the offensive. "Furthermore, my master wishes to know what has become of a Pennsylvania trader named John Trotter and his servant, James McLaughlin, who were captured with all their goods."

Captain de Repentigny answered that question. "These men were sent to Canada, but they have now returned home, I believe."

"By what authority did you capture and make prisoners of English subjects?" George demanded.

"Sir, the country belongs to His Most Christian Majesty. No Englishman has a right to trade upon the waters of the Ohio. We have orders to make prisoners of all who do," de Repentigny explained.

George had his answer to Dinwiddie's letter in that statement. The French would not give up the land of the Ohio.

At that moment, the door burst open and

Tanacharison, Jeskakake, and White Thunder strode in. The orderly apologized to his commander, "Sir, they insisted . . ."

"We are delighted to see our children anytime," St. Pierre said calmly. "It is quite all right, Orderly. Come, gentlemen, come in. I am Sieur Legardeur de St. Pierre, sent by your father, King Louis, and Governor Duquesne. What a great pleasure to greet you at last. The governor himself has told me much about you and sends his warmest greetings. Orderly, chairs for our Iroquois children." The old man bowed and then embraced each chief. "Come, we must toast this great occasion. Orderly, brandy for our guests." St. Pierre seemed to have forgotten all about the Englishmen.

Then he looked up and stared at them with his one cold eye. "Monsieurs, if you would excuse us, we have business with the great men of the Iroquois."

"I'll bet you have," George said under his breath. But to St. Pierre he could only bow and leave the room.

George was gleeful as he crossed the parade ground. "He did it, Mr. Gist, Tanacharison did it. He forced St. Pierre to see him. As soon as I get the written reply to Dinwiddie's letter, we can leave. I am going to take St. Pierre up on the offer of the canoes. We can move much faster on water. I will send Currin and Jenkins this very day back to Venango with the weak horses to wait for us."

"Do you think it is wise to split the party? There are so few of us." Gist seemed alarmed.

"Time is important, Mr. Gist. I must get back to Williamsburg."

Gist looked at George doubtfully, but said no more.

After the horses had been dispatched with Currin and Jenkins, George realized Tanacharison had been with St. Pierre a long time. He began to feel anxious. George paced the floor of his room, often opening the door and looking toward headquarters.

It was dark when a knock came at last. George opened the door to find Davison and Tanacharison on the threshold. "Tanacharison, I have been waiting for you," George blurted out. "You have news?"

Pleasure and anger were the only two emotions Tanacharison ever permitted himself to display. Now his handsome face showed neither. Through Davison he said, "I offered belts with signs of towns on them to St. Pierre as de Marin had demanded. But St. Pierre said he does not want them. He wants the treaty belts to stay in force. He wants it as a sign of peace and great friendship and trade with my people. He said he would send goods to Logstown—many canoes full."

"Logstown!" George cried. "Mr. Gist, Mr. Davison, they intend to take Logstown, too! It is our last outpost beyond the Allegheny Mountains."

"The French mean to capture the last of the traders or chase them back over the mountains!" Davison exclaimed. "If Logstown goes like Venango, there will not be an English trader on the River Ohio."

Then Tanacharison broke into the conversation. "Don't want French at Logstown. We trade with English. Goods better. English ask less furs," Davison hurriedly translated.

George was startled. Tanacharison's words were encouraging, but saying them at that moment was almost as if he had understood what the Englishmen had been talking about among themselves. George looked at the chief curiously, but the question left his head when another knock came at the door.

A French soldier saluted stiffly. "Commandant Washington, Sieur de St. Pierre asks you to come to his headquarters."

"At once!" George answered, not wishing to waste any time. Out into the snow George, Gist, and Van Braam went without cloaks. They quickly trotted across the parade ground to St. Pierre's headquarters.

Captain Picard greeted them. "Commandant, you have come so quickly. Let me first announce you to Sieur de St. Pierre. One moment."

"Thank you. Merci." George answered in one of the few words of French he had been able to pick up.

The captain entered St. Pierre's office and

then poked his head out again. "Commandant, Monsieurs. Sieur de St. Pierre will see you now."

"Ah, Commandant Washington, thank you for coming so promptly even though the hour is late." St. Pierre gave a hint of a smile. "But I know you are anxious to begin your return journey. Therefore, my fellow officers and I have written a reply to your honored Governor's letter with all possible, but careful, haste. Here it is." With that, St. Pierre handed George a folded paper with the wax seal of France on the back. George would not be able to open it. No matter, he was sure he knew what it said.

"On behalf of my government and myself, I thank you and your officers for their attention and speed," George said.

"Not at all, Commandant, not at all. We each must be the best servants to our kings we can possibly be, n'est pas?" (is it not so?)

"Now as I said the other day, I have placed two canoes at your disposal which I will stock with provisions so you can leave at first light tomorrow. Although it is some forty leagues to Venango by water, I know you will be more comfortable going that way. Commissary La Force has told me of the dreadful time you had getting here across a great swamp. Dreadful! Dreadful!" St. Pierre cast his one eye heavenward as he prattled on in rapid French.

After listening to the interpretation, George ordered Van Braam, "Tell the commander I and my companions thank him for his great kindness, his careful attention to Governor Dinwiddie's letter, and his gifts of canoes and provisions." George executed his best bow. "Be sure my government will be most indebted to him."

"Not at all, Commandant. Now I bid you bonsoir and wish you a good rest before starting your long journey."

"Merci, merci!" George replied.

After breakfast the Englishmen strolled out the gate of Fort Le Boeuf and down to the banks of French Creek. Much to George's surprise, casks of food and spirits along with blankets and small kettles were piled at the river's edge. Soldiers were stowing the supplies in the large canoes.

"Well, Major, St. Pierre is living up to his word. Canoes plus food and supplies. Fine wine for us to drink as we drift lazily down French Creek amid the ice flows," Gist joked.

"Oh, I thought the spirits were to pour on the ice in the river so as to melt it as we pass," George replied, falling in with Gist's humor. "I think we must go and thank St. Pierre for his kindness."

"Mr. Davison, find the chiefs and be sure they are ready to leave," George ordered.

Steward broke in. "It ain't likely they are goin' any place."

"What do you mean, Mr. Steward? The Indians go with us."

"I seen them French officers talkin' to them yesterday and last night. They been givin' 'em all kinds o' presents and promises. They have the best guest quarters in the fort. Better n' yours, Major. With lots o' food and spirits. They're tryin' t' keep them all winter."

"What? The chiefs have to leave with us. The whole English alliance with the Six Nations depends upon them staying with us. Where is Tanacharison? I will not have this. He is coming with me or else! Come, Mr. Davison."

"The chiefs are in their quarters, I think," offered Steward.

George started off with his giant stride. Within minutes, he was pounding on the door of the quarters of Tanacharison, Jeskakake, and White Thunder.

When Tanacharison opened the door, George forced a smile on his face. "Good morning. I have come to tell you the canoes are ready to go."

Tanacharison evaded George's eyes. "No go today."

"Why?" George insisted.

"French father St. Pierre say his children cannot go yet. Go tomorrow. Have more talk this day."

"But you promised you would escort me always in the forest. And you know I must leave to return with much speed to your brother, Dinwiddie. If I were to go alone and some Ottawas killed me, how would you explain to Dinwiddie you broke your promise?" Despite the cold, George felt sweat running down his back. To pressure Tanacharison this way was dangerous.

"Go tomorrow!" Tanacharison said and turned away.

George knew further talk was useless. He left Tanacharison's room and headed across the parade grounds to St. Pierre's headquarters.

George swept past the sputtering Picard and knocked at St. Pierre's door before boldly opening it.

"Commandant Washington! You have come to say au revoir (good-bye). But we were intending to see you off at the riverbank. But no matter. Come, we will all have a brandy together, a farewell toast."

"Mr. Van Braam," George ordered, "Ask Sieur Legardeur de St. Pierre when he will finish his business with the representatives of the Iroquois."

"But I have no further business with the chiefs." St. Pierre pretended surprise at George's question when put to him by Van Braam.

"They say you will not let them leave. This treatment to an emissary of a friendly government is not to be borne. To delay them is to delay me, for they are part of my party. You promised you would forward my journey as much as possible. And since I thought you a gentleman, I took you at your word," George said, staring into the equally angry eye of St. Pierre.

But St. Pierre's words belied what George read in that single eye. "Commandant Washington, I have supplied my two best canoes. They await your departure. I do not know why the chiefs linger." He shrugged his shoulders in the Gallic manner. "But they are old men like me and the cold makes our bones creak. We long for a warm hearth. A young fellow like you does not know of these things yet."

George burned under the words about his youth. St. Pierre was treating him like a child. He turned on his heel and walked out.

As he left the headquarters, he found Steward and Davison waiting for him. "We got somethin' to tell you, Major. We been listenin' around and we found out the French promised the Indians a present of guns if they'd stay till tomorrow mornin'."

"Guns!" George boomed.

"The Frenchmen are desperate, Major!" Gist said.

George took a few heavy steps, turned, and walked back. "The craftiness of the French! It is just as Dinwiddie said, 'They smile in your face, shrug their shoulders, and put a knife in your back.' Damn them! I'm going to talk to Tanacharison again."

For the second time this early morning, he knocked at the door. But this time he did not smile. When the door opened, George pushed his way inside. "Tanacharison, the French father has promised you a present of guns. This is true?"

This time Tanacharison looked him in the eyes. "Yes. My people need guns. Bow and arrow good. Tomahawk good, but not against guns."

George had to agree with Tanacharison. A gun was a precious possession to him. Finally, he said, "After you get the guns, then what?"

"We wait one day. The French will give us guns tomorrow. Then we go back to Logstown, protect you as I said." Davison translated the Indian's promise.

George hesitated, thinking, "If I stay one more day, I will please Tanacharison. They will get their guns and leave with us. I will lose only time. If I stay and the French do not give the guns, then I can accuse them of breaking their word to the chiefs. It will make the French look bad. It is worth a try." Then he asked, "Will you leave in the canoes with me tomorrow morning whether you get the guns or no?"

"I go," Tanacharison said at last.

"I have your word as a Hodenosaunee?" George demanded.

"You have my promise."

"Until tomorrow then."

Tanacharison nodded.

The Englishmen went back to their own quarters to wait out the long day and night. But George did not tell Christopher Gist or the others of his plan to accuse the French of lying before the Indians if they did not present the guns. Only he lived with the knowledge that this day might be their last twenty-four hours alive.

It was midmorning before all the soldiers and officers of Fort Le Boeuf, dressed in their best uniforms, were on the parade ground. Captain Picard, Commissary La Force, and most of the officers stood in front of the troops. Fifes sounded, drums rolled, and officers shouted commands as their soldiers drilled. Tanacharison, White Thunder, Jeskakake, and Guyasuta watched.

So did the Englishmen. "Quite a show they're putting on," George remarked.

"I don't see the guns," Gist whispered. "I don't see St. Pierre or de Repentigny either. I wonder what tricks they are up to today."

"Probably a way to get rid of us," George answered with a certain satisfaction in knowing he was causing the French so much trouble.

However, when the grandiose military drill was over, St. Pierre and de Repentigny came out of the headquarters bastion each carrying two guns.

"Mr. Davison," George asked quietly, "Listen carefully and tell me what they are saying."

"They say they want their dear children to stay the winter with them where they will be warm and have much food. In the spring, they can have many canoes. They will send food today by canoe to all the villages."

"What is Tanacharison saying?"

"He thanks them but says he must return to his people." Davison continued, "St. Pierre says these guns are but the symbols of the great love the French father and all Frenchmen have for them. Should they want for anything, anything at all, they must come to the fort and ask. It is a place of refuge from enemies for their women and children."

"The guns. The guns," George urged under his breath as he watched St. Pierre.

The drums beat a long, slow roll.

"There they go! They are presenting the guns!" Gist shouted excitedly.

"Thank God!" George exclaimed. He had won. No need now to put his dangerous plan into action. He started toward the chiefs to escort them to the waiting canoes without further delay.

Just then, an orderly handed a bottle and some tin cups to St. Pierre. He poured brandy and held it toward the Indians.

"Oh no, he doesn't!" George started running. "You have your guns, Tanacharison. Now you must live up to your promise. We must leave now!" St. Pierre and de Repentigny glared angrily at this upstart boy destroying their plans. Tanacharison started to lift his hand in anger toward George. But George looked into Tanacharison's eyes, level with his own, and would not allow himself so much as a blink. He could feel a power rising in him as he held Tanacharison's squinting gaze. George was no longer afraid of Tanacharison even though at any moment he expected a blow from the mighty Seneca chief.

St. Pierre held out the bottle and the cup invitingly. George could smell the strong spirits even in the cold open air. He knew Tanacharison must smell them, too. George had no doubt if the chiefs took even one drink, they would not be able to steer the canoes through the wild waters of French Creek. Two drinks and they would fall down in drunken stupors and all would be lost.

"Tell him again we must leave now," George ordered Davison. "He promised me as soon as he had the guns, we would go. Together. Remind him, Mr. Davison!"

Davison's voice was shaky as he repeated the words in Seneca.

"Great man of the Hodenosaunees, you promised!" George shouted in Seneca. He did not even realize the words had come out, for he did not remember learning them in the past few weeks.

Suddenly, Tanacharison raised his powerful arm and held the gun above his head like a trophy. "We go!" Turning, he walked majestically toward the river. George followed, holding himself straight and tall as he walked past the hundred soldiers standing at attention. His heart pounded and he wanted to run, but he forced himself to keep on and not look to see if the French were aiming their guns at his back.

When they reached the canoes, Gist, Van Braam, and Davison scrambled in. Steward, forward in the canoe, held his paddle ready to strike the water. MacQuire pressed his hands against the stern, prepared to launch the craft into the creek.

But George waited on the shore watching the Indians settle into the other canoe. The young warrior Guyasuta stood ready to push off. With a last look of triumph toward St. Pierre, George folded himself into his canoe. "Push off!" he ordered. The canoes slid across the sand; the paddles dug deep into the icy water.

Chapter Eight

Conotocarious

Sunday, December 16, 1753—French Creek

George dug his paddle into the water and pushed with the powerful muscles of his shoulders and arms again and again. He wanted to put distance between himself and Fort Le Boeuf as fast as possible. The canoe wobbled about in the swift current, threatening to turn turtle at any moment as the six Englishmen fought to control it. The three old chiefs and the young hunter in the other canoe quickly fell into harmony with the river and in minutes were out of sight downstream.

Steward turned around and looked at George strangely several times. Soon Gist suggested, "Major, why don't you and Mr. Van Braam save your strength. In this current, four paddlers are enough."

George had become well aware in less than ten minutes that paddling the large canoe required much skill. He also knew Gist was telling him that he and Jacob were slowing instead of speeding the progress of the frail craft.

Pulling his paddle out of the water, he held it across the top of the canoe in front of him as he studied Steward and Davison. He watched how deeply they put the paddles into the water, at what angle, how long their sweep. After awhile, he carefully turned himself around to where he could watch Gist and MacQuire behind him. He became almost hypnotized by the unity of the paddlers' motion, and he began to feel it in his own body. After a time, he picked up his paddle again, positioned his hands on it just as Steward did, and dug into the water. The canoe moved faster. Steward turned around again, and this time he grinned.

At dusk, the canoe was beached and the Englishmen made camp for the night. George's muscles ached in places he did not know he had any. Taking off his gloves, he found blisters on his hands. But the next day he did his full share of paddling even though every stroke was painful.

Shortly after midday, Steward stopped and pointed toward something on the shore. George saw the Indians' canoe was drawn up on the bank. "Make for the shore," George ordered.

As the canoe went aground in the mud, the Englishmen scrambled out and up the riverbank. At the top, they found a campfire, the remains of food, but no Indians. "Where do you think they are, Mr. Gist? Do you think some mishap befell them?" George was worried.

Gist and the traders studied the snow-covered ground around the camp. Finally, he said,

"I see no sign of trouble. They may be hunting or scouting."

"Do you think they might have gone back to Fort Le Boeuf or maybe decided to go over-land to Venango?" George asked.

"I doubt it, but you never know. Shall we push on?" Gist suggested.

George was still worried about the Indians. "I want to stay here and see if they return, Mr. Gist. Besides, we need the rest ourselves."

Gist looked at him strangely. "Rest? From what?" he asked. "I thought you could not lose a minute getting back to Williamsburg."

George felt foolish. He realized traders paddled for days, weeks at a time. He was ex-hausted after just a day and a half. "We will wait," he insisted. They set to work building up the fire to ward off the cold. About three hours later, Tanacharison appeared, soon followed by Guyasuta and old Jeskakake. The men were elated as they dragged three dead bears into camp.

"Guns good," old Jeskakake said, patting the polished stock with one wizened hand. "Jeskakake got one bear."

George shook his head in wonder at the old man. He could not imagine how the ancient had even managed to lift the gun into firing position, much less bring down a bear.

The Indians set about butchering the animals and dressing the skins. Guyasuta held the skin of his bear up still dripping blood. "Fine fur. Good for winter."

"Will you trade it?" Tanacharison asked.

"No. For me," Guyasuta answered.

George became curious as he watched them. He had seen animals butchered before on his father's farms, but these men did it differently. It seemed almost a ceremony and sometimes they sang or chanted.

That night they all feasted on bear meat, all they could eat. George had come to realize that starvation during winter was an ever-present threat to the forest people. Therefore, he did not gorge himself although the Indians ate until they were sick. When they finished at last, they carefully packed the remaining meat away, again chanting softly.

"Mr. Gist, why do they sing over the meat?"

"I guess they are happy they made a kill and have enough to eat for once."

George was not satisfied with the answer. Finally, he told Davison to ask Tanacharison.

The chief looked at George as if he were rather stupid. "We must pay great honor to these bears who allowed themselves to be killed today. Other animals watch. If we not give honor to their bodies and spirits, other animals not allow themselves be killed. The people starve. We thank animals many times for their sacrifice."

George pondered these ideas. He remembered the stories of lambs sacrificed in the Bible.

Soon the Englishmen rolled up in their blankets atop layers of pine branches and quickly went to sleep. But the Indians did not sleep. Restlessly, they stared into the black forest and talked among themselves. When morning came, they were still only three. White Thunder had not returned to camp. Tanacharison sat puffing his long pipe as he stared into the campfire as if it might tell him something.

Now the Englishmen conferred. George stated his position. "I do not want to be separated from Tanacharison again. Sometime in the next few days, we will reach Venango and Captain Joncaire will be waiting. Besides, I think we could help by forming a search party. There are six of us and only three of them."

But Steward brought up an old problem— the weather. "Major, maybe ya noticed we ain't had rain nor snow fer four days now. I was lookin' at the river n' it's fallin' fast. If we stay t' help, we might not be able t' float the canoe. If we can't, well, we ain't got no horses . . ."

"And it's getting colder. The creek with low water will freeze more quickly," Gist pointed out.

George rubbed his hands over his eyes. Slowly he turned and went to Tanacharison. "Mr. Davison, ask Tanacharison if we can help him look for White Thunder. He has been gone all night. I am concerned for him."

Tanacharison looked for a long moment at George. Then he said, "White Thunder will come back. We wait."

"But the river is falling and we must go while the canoes can still float. Let us look for White Thunder. Perhaps he is hurt and cannot return to camp."

But Tanacharison misunderstood him for he said angrily, "We will not go. Wait for White Thunder."

When Davison interpreted his words, George said soothingly, "I know you must wait for White Thunder. That is good. But I must go on if we cannot help you. You come then when White Thunder returns. We will meet you in Venango."

Tanacharison nodded his head and walked away.

"All right, gentlemen, let us be off," George sighed, still looking after Tanacharison.

For the first time in nearly two months, George prayed for rain to raise the level of the river. Several times he and his companions had to get out and stand waist deep in icy water for half an hour to guide the heavily loaded canoe over sandbars. Then they climbed back in and began paddling again while their clothes froze to their bodies.

On the third day, they were pounding the ice around the canoe to make a passage when Steward in the bow called out, "There's a sharp bend ahead. It's blocked solid with ice. I think we got t' portage."

Groans went up from George and the others as they guided the canoe into the bank. George sat down on a log for he was very tired and shivering violently. "We are going to build a fire. MacQuire, scout the river below here and see what the shortest route to open water is. We are not going to waste our strength carrying this damn canoe a foot farther than we have to."

Soon a big fire burned and the men stood close to it drying their clothes. George broke out a bottle of French brandy to warm their insides. They swallowed the fiery spirits as George offered a toast. "Merci, Sieur de St. Pierre."

In an hour, MacQuire returned from his scouting mission. "The creek is open again over there," he said, pointing in a southwesterly direction.

"How far, Mr. MacQuire?"

"Bout a quarter o' a mile."

"All right, everyone, let's go." George went to the canoe and put his hands on it prepared to carry his share. He looked across at Christopher Gist, who was about to pick up the other side. "So you really believe, Sir, the French can get from Montreal all the way to New Orleans paddling one of these contraptions? Maybe even out to those Shining Mountains?"

"So THEY say."

"They are liars, Mr. Gist. There is no way anyone, even a Frenchman could survive in one of these handiworks of the devil." George longed to kick the canoe, but he knew he would only put a gaping hole in its flimsy side and add to their woes.

They carried the canoe overland and launched it again in French Creek. After going about five miles farther downstream, they heard human voices other than their own in the wilderness. Instantly, Steward and MacQuire steadied the canoe bow and stern. George, Gist, Davison, and Van Braam reached for their guns. Their eyes swept the dense trees and thickets along the riverbank that could have concealed an army. Suddenly, Gist exclaimed, "Will you look what is coming behind us!"

Through the passage the Englishmen had broken in the ice came four more canoes. In the lead canoe were the Indians, four of them. The three other vessels were crowded with Frenchmen. As they sped by, waving, George recognized Commissary La Force.

Grimly, George watched them as they paddled hard and were soon out of sight again. "So St. Pierre is not done with his game yet. Dig in, fellows, we cannot leave the Indians in the company of the French. We must catch up."

And catch up they did the next day as they came upon an overturned French canoe. Men were in the water trying to right it. The remaining two canoes circled around trying to pick up the bottles and casks of spirits that bobbed in the creek. The Indians were nowhere in sight.

Steward turned around and looked questioningly at George. Grinning broadly, he waved Steward on. They dug their paddles into the black water harder than ever and ran by the floundering Frenchmen.

As they approached Venango at last, George decided he wanted to be rid of the canoe. With his surveyor's eye, he estimated that the way from Fort Le Boeuf to Venango by way of the meandering French Creek was several times farther than by land.

As the six Englishmen beached the canoe, they were happy to see Barnaby Currin and William Jenkins waiting for them on the shore. Neither looked as if he had been molested by the French. But Barnaby greeted George with other bad news. "We lost two more horses, Major. I'm mighty sorry. They just keeled over."

"I am sorry, too, Mr. Currin. I know you did your best. With the one we lost on the way to Fort Le Boeuf, that means we are out three."

"The ones left are not good neither, Major."

"The rest here at Venango has not helped strengthen them?" George asked.

"No fresh forage, Sir. We gave them some of the oats ye brought along, but it's getting moldy."

George called all the men together and presented the choices to them. "Mr. Currin says the pack horses are in poor condition. That leaves us the choice of traveling by water farther. But after the last six days in the canoe, I consider it a dangerous way and no faster."

"The water is falling, too," Christopher Gist pointed out.

"And freezing over," Henry Steward added. "It would mean more portages."

"It seems we must use the horses then," George concluded. His seven companions could not offer any other ideas.

"Very well." George squinted up at the sky. "It is too late to leave today much as I wish to be away from Venango. And I must consult with Tanacharison. Mr. Davison, find out what has become of the Indians and ask Tanacharison to come to me."

Davison went in search of the chief while George and the other members of the expedition unloaded the canoe and transferred their supplies to Currin and Jenkins's camp. When Davison reappeared an hour later, he said mysteriously, "Major, Tanacharison wants to talk to you over in the trees there."

George put down the bag he was carrying and followed Davison. They found Tanacharison waiting. George was tired and could not be bothered with making polite talk. "Mr. Davison, ask the chief if he wants to go overland or wishes to continue down the Allegheny to the River Ohio and on to Logstown?"

Davison spoke in Seneca to Tanacharison and then repeated his answer to George. "He says he will have to go by canoe because White Thunder is badly hurt. He cannot walk."

"I am sorry to hear White Thunder has been hurt. I have medicines with me. I am not a doctor, but perhaps my medicines can help."

"Tanacharison says no. They will care for White Thunder. They will stay here until he is better and able to travel."

George's fatigue turned to exasperation when he heard Tanacharison wanted to wait—again. "Joncaire has gotten to him already, I see. I'll just bet White Thunder is sick," he thought. "Tell Tanacharison this. I am sorry White Thunder is ill. The Delawares here could care for him. But we must leave."

Tanacharison's reply was stubborn. "I will not leave White Thunder."

George sighed. He was so weary of this struggle to hold the Indians against the French. So weary of this duel that never seemed to end. The hell with it. "I must leave you then. I must go back to Governor Dinwiddie and tell him what his friend, Tanacharison, has done and said. He will be sorry you cannot come with me yourself."

"I cannot go with you now. I will try to meet you at Forks and give you a speech for Dinwiddie," Tanacharison said through Davison.

For a moment, George was surprised by the offer, but he was not about to be taken in by it.

He felt Tanacharison was putting him off. How would they ever meet in this vast, godforsaken wilderness?

Then Tanacharison said, "I will send Guyasuta with you. Help get meat."

George was touched by this offer. Somehow he knew it was sincere. Tanacharison, in his way, was trying to fulfill his promises. But he could not accept Guyasuta for he realized that if White Thunder was really crippled, Tanacharison and old Jeskakake would need the young man to help them. "Thank you. Guyasuta is a fine hunter, but I could not take him from your service. We will be all right," he said, in as polite a refusal as he could think of.

Then George threw caution aside and burst out, "Tanacharison, be on your guard against the French. They only mean to do great mischief to you and your people with their spirits and flattery and fine speeches." It was a last desperate attempt to save the English alliance with the Six Nations and to warn this man he had come to respect of the destruction he could see coming for the forest people.

When Davison translated George's plea, Tanacharison said a few words and Davison started to walk away.

Alarmed, George asked, "Where are you going, Mr. Davison? We are not finished yet."

"Tanacharison told me to go."

"I, too?" George wondered if his words had

angered the chief. He immediately regretted his outburst. Letting anger and frustration make him lose his iron self-control had ruined everything.

But Davison said, "No, you are to stay. He wishes to talk to you alone."

"But I cannot understand Nundawao (Seneca) or Hodenosaunee," protested George.

Davison shrugged his shoulders and started walking again.

"Washington, I know Joncaire. He cannot fool me. Joncaire born Frenchman, a Nundawao (Seneca) by choice. His clan useful to Hodenosaunee. I have cared for my people much time. I know what I must do," Tanacharison said in English.

He must have seen the bewilderment in George's face. He reached out and put a hand on each of George's broad shoulders. "You are strong boy. Maybe some day you become great warrior. Then as your years increase, your people make you chief, like me. You sit at council fire of your people."

George looked down in confusion. He could not help but be pleased at this praise. Despite his youth, he had won some admiration from the great chief. If only he would remain loyal to the English.

Tanacharison spoke again. "You our true brother. From now on among all the people of the Hodenosaunee, you called Conotocarious."

"Tanacharison . . ." Words failed George. Ever since he had heard Gist called Annosanah, he had longed to have an Indian name. He had even thought of making one up for himself, but he knew in his heart it must be earned. Conotocarious. Somewhere he had heard that name before. In his mind he went back ten years, even more—back to before his father died. Augustine Washington used to tell George and his brothers and sister about the Washington family. How their great-grandfather John and his brother Lawrence had been forced to leave England. They were loyal to King Charles I who lost the English Civil War to Oliver Cromwell in 1645. But when their ship reached Virginia, they at once saw the opportunities the New World had to offer. With hard work, they acquired large landholdings. John became a member of the House of Burgesses and a colonel in the Virginia militia. When there was an Indian uprising, he fought fiercely. One night he invited five Algonquian chiefs to come to his camp to discuss peace terms. When they came, he ruthlessly murdered all five. Then he burned their villages. From then on, the Indians called him Conotocarious. "But how did you know, Tanacharison, that the Algonquians gave my great-grandfather that name almost a hundred years ago?"

Tanacharison looked at George with his great eyes like ageless brown pools. He said, "Englishmen, Frenchmen write on papers. We no need papers. We have shamans, men who re-member everything that happens and tell our people."

"But my great-grandfather did a great in-justice to your people. I have not done injustice to your people. Why do you call me a 'burner of villages'?"

"They not my people. They Algonquian, not Hodenosaunee. You known as Clan Wash-ington among your people. Clan Conotocarious among mine. When you do great deed, I give you new name to be known among the Hoden-osaunee. But make Conotocarious a name of honor while you live, Washington," he warned. Then Tanacharison started to walk away.

"Tanacharison," George called after him. "We will meet again—great brother."

The chief turned and looked at George one more time.

"Aguyase!"

Chapter Nine

The Assassin

Sunday, December 23, 1753—On the Trail to Murdering Town

With first light, the Englishmen broke camp for all were anxious to be away from Venango. As they started on the trail south of the town, George took one last look at the hated French fleurs-de-lis flapping over John Frazier's house. "I hope I never have to see that flag again. But I am afraid only war will bring it down."

All day the men and horses slipped and slid over the icy trail. George watched anxiously as the weak animals struggled under their burdens. When the early twilight of late December came upon them, George called a halt to make camp for the night. They had traveled only five miles since dawn.

The next morning, before the horses were loaded, George gave an order. "The riding horses are to be loaded to relieve some of the burden on the pack horses. All of us will walk except the drivers, Currin and Steward, who must ride." No one complained for everyone knew the problems as well as George.

Yet new problems beset them. Snow began to fall harder and harder. Within a short time, the snow was ankle deep, then knee deep. Hour after hour men and horses plodded on, slower and slower, this day and the next. Although they had little breath to spare, Christopher Gist said, "Merry Christmas, Major."

George looked at him. "You jest, Sir!"

"Don't you wish we were in Williamsburg? I can see the candles in the windows, smell the roasting goose, taste the pies." Gist went on. "The balls and assemblies, huh, Major? I'll bet a young buck like you is a devil with the ladies."

"I do not think I have ever danced a more fancy reel than I am doing right now trying to keep my footing on this ice and snow."

"Do you like dancing, Major?" Gist asked.

"I do indeed, Mr. Gist."

"And the hot, spiced punch to sip between sets. Think of it, Major."

George could smell the cinnamon and cloves wafting up from the wassail bowls, could see the tables set with cakes and jellies. "I am surprised you think of Williamsburg, Mr. Gist. I would imagine your thoughts would be with your family on the Yadkin River down in Carolina. I am sorry I have taken you away from them. I truly did not expect to be so long on this journey. Dinwiddie expected me back in a month. Ha!"

"No matter, Major. I have been absent from home at Christmas often the last few years. In 1750, I spent Christmas Day at Muskingum with the Wyandot Indians. George Croghan had a stout trading post there."

"George Croghan seems to be everywhere," George commented.

Gist went on. "Since there were a number of white traders there, I sent word around I would read prayers to mark the day of our Lord's birth. Well, traders being a mostly ungodly lot, few came to my little service. But some Indians did attend. I read some sermons of the Church of England which my traveling companion, Andrew Montour, translated into the Wyandot language. The Indians were truly interested in what I said. They invited me to live among them, baptize their children, perform marriage ceremonies, and teach them about Christianity. I was most touched, but, of course, I could not stay as I was on government business again."

"That is when they gave you the name Annosanah?" George asked.

"Oh, I bore you. I am sorry. Repeating stories is a sign of one's old age, is it not?"

"You have never finished the story, Mr. Gist. Since it is a Christmas story, what better time than today."

"But it is not a joyful Christmas story," Gist warned.

"Tell me."

"The next day, a prisoner, a white woman, tried to escape. The Indians recaptured her. Then they beat her with clubs. When she fell senseless to the ground, they hacked off her head. We white men could only stand by and watch. We were powerless to save one of our own for we would have suffered the same fate. Barnaby Currin buried her that night." Gist's voice was full of bitterness.

George was silent. He did not look at Christopher Gist, but he now understood him a little better.

Christmas night was bitterly cold. When the camp on Great Beaver Creek awoke the next morning, Steward, Jenkins, and MacQuire could not get up. "I got frostbite, Major. Both feet and my fingers," Steward said.

George examined all three men. "We must get a large fire going and build some sort of shelter. The tent is not enough," he ordered. Quickly, they began the hard search for more dry wood. Currin, Davison, and Van Braam fashioned a lean-to. Gist brought extra coverings and helped the afflicted men to a place close to the fire. Born of their total self-reliance, the three frostbitten men began to treat themselves.

The whole expedition dug in to wait for better weather. But George drew Christopher Gist aside. "These men cannot walk for several days. They could get gangrene and lose their hands and feet. The horses are too weak to carry them. They must stay here until they can travel."

Gist nodded his head in agreement. George continued, "I have been thinking. Even if we could push on today or tomorrow, we can only travel as fast as the horses. There is no chance of our getting to Williamsburg in a reasonable time. I propose that you and I carry what we can and go ahead on foot to Murdering Town. Then go across country to the Allegheny River, cross on the ice, and go to John Frazier's at Turtle Creek. We could get fresh horses there."

"What about the others?" Gist asked with deep concern.

"The men can take their time. Go by way of Logstown. Currin can guide them from here, can he not?"

"Yes, he can, but my God, Major, you don't know what you are proposing. There is no possibility we could make it alone."

"We have compasses. You know the territory generally. We will make it."

"I do not fear becoming lost. It is you, Major. I must remind you, you are a gentleman used to riding a horse. You are unaccustomed to walking long distances in the woods especially through deep snow. You could not survive. Let me go alone. I have done it before," Gist urged. "I will get the letter to Williamsburg and let Dinwiddie know you are coming."

George's quick temper burst out of control at what he thought was an insult. Gist all but called him a silly dandy, a tenderfoot. Had not he been through enough on this journey? What more did he have to do to prove himself? "Let me remind you, Mr. Gist, that although you have more experience, I am half your age. I was put in charge of this expedition by the Governor and the Council, not you. We will do what I think best. If you do not wish to go with me, I will go alone. But I will go! And I will get back to Williamsburg by any means possible."

Their eyes locked in an angry stare. But George's stinging words silenced the older man's warnings. "You still mean to get yourself killed for the Ohio Company, don't you? Well, if I may be permitted to make one suggestion, SIR! Put on Indian dress. Boots and a cloak will never make it through the woods. Come, I will lend you some of mine since we are of a size."

The two men collected clothing for George. Near the fire, he pulled off his boots and drew on leather leggings over his knee breeches. After adding two pairs of homespun woolen stockings, he wiggled his feet into deerhide moccasins which he laced up above his ankles. He put on his own hunting jacket. Gist gave him a warm matchcoat made of the furs of small animals sewed together. It reached only halfway down his long legs.

When George had finished outfitting himself, he called the party together and told them of his plan. The traders looked at Gist in alarm. Gist avoided their eyes. Jacob Van Braam pleaded to go with George. "What if you meet more French?" he reasoned. He did not want to remain in the company of the Scotch-Irish traders who barely tolerated the Dutchman.

"Mr. Van Braam, I am putting you in charge of the expedition because of your military experience," George said, looking at the traders so they would not abandon Van Braam. "You are to bring the horses and follow the trail to Logstown, then follow the river to John Frazier's. I will leave instructions for you there. Here is money to purchase anything you need."

"Mr. Davison, here are your wages and a bit more to serve as interpreter for Mr. Van Braam until he leaves Logstown."

The trader smiled his toothless grin when he saw the silver George had promised him in the palm of his hand at last.

"And Mr. Davison, I thank you. I could not have managed without you."

"Any time, Major, I can work for you again, I'd be proud."

George then turned to Barnaby Currin. "Can you guide the party back to Frazier's, Mr. Currin, when the men are well?"

"Aye, Major. You kin count on Barnaby Currin."

"Thank you, Mr. Currin. Thank all of you." George distributed their wages and shook hands all around.

While George spoke to the men, Gist fashioned knapsacks for their papers, ammunition, and some food. He tied one on George's back and put the other pack on his own shoulders. Picking up their guns, George and Christopher Gist waved farewell.

"Godspeed," the traders called.

The two men started down the trail to Murdering Town. They were soon blurred and then swallowed up by the blowing snow. They walked as fast as the ice on the trail permitted. The cold wind stung their throats and lungs, and George soon was gasping. He buried his face in the fur of his coat to warm his breath, but he could not get enough air. They became thirsty from their struggle, but the streams they crossed were too frozen to yield even a sip of water. Before long, George realized Christopher Gist had only meant to be kind when he tried to talk him out of this undertaking. His feet were soon sore and his legs felt like trunks of trees as he dragged them along one step at a time.

The early night came, but they kept walking. George did not utter one word of complaint as he forced himself to keep up.

Suddenly, Gist stopped. "I think I see a cabin through the trees."

"Are you sure?" George grasped at his words.

Gist hurried on. The cabin was about a hundred yards away when he stopped again.

"Is it deserted?" George whispered, for he could see no lighted candles or smoke coming from the chimney.

"It's an Indian cabin. It looks deserted but we will circle around," Gist said. Just as they had approached Frazier's, he stayed hidden in the trees as he studied the cabin from all sides.

"Look! The door is open," George said. "In this cold, if anyone were in there, the door would be closed, certainly."

The two men broke out of the trees and hurried to the cabin. George collapsed on the floor. He had not an ounce of strength left. "I think we covered some twenty miles today."

"Good," Gist said. He started a fire.

"Isn't that dangerous?" George asked. "We might attract attention."

"We need warmth and food and water or we will die anyway," Gist reasoned.

After eating a makeshift meal and drinking melted snow, the two men rolled up in their matchcoats close to the fire and slept. It was after midnight when Gist shook George awake. "Major, how are you feeling?"

"Tolerable. Why?" George asked sleepily.

"If you are able, we should move on."

George moved his legs. The muscles were painful, but they felt strong again. He struggled to his feet. The two men put on their coats and packs. Picking up their guns, they left the cabin and plunged into the woods.

By midmorning, the telltale smell of smoke in the air told them they must be approaching the Indian village of Murdering Town. George felt the tingle of fear again that he had known when he entered Logstown. How would they be received by these people? Were they friendly to the English, or were they French Indians? He had no presents to give them; there was no room in his knapsack. He did not speak of his fears to his companion, but when they sighted the first wigwam, he let Gist go first. His fears were not relieved when he saw a number of men emerge from the longhouses and cabins and come toward them. "What are they, Mr. Gist?" George asked nervously.

"Delawares," Gist answered, holding up his hands as a sign of peace. "Aguyase!" he called.

"Annosanah! Aguyase! Welcome!" One of the men stepped forward to greet them. "And Conotocarious. Welcome!"

"Conotocarious?" Gist asked, looking at George questioningly.

"Tanacharison gave me that name before we parted in Venango. News travels fast out here." But secretly, George was very pleased that he was now known as Conotocarious among the people of the forest.

"Annosanah, where are your horses, men? Something bad happen?"

Gist frowned as he studied the man. He did not answer.

But George did. He was so pleased to find someone friendly and who spoke English to boot, he felt he should return the gesture of friendship. "The horses were weak and slow. Some men were sick. We came on alone."

"When leave Venango? How many days?" the Indian persisted. "Men come to Murdering Town soon?"

Gist put a hand on George's arm to stop him. "It doesn't matter," he said. "Who are you? I think we have met before."

"No! We never meet. But I hear much about great Annosanah."

Flattery did not impress Gist.

George broke in. "Do you know the shortest way to the crossing of the Allegheny near the forks?"

"I know way. Take two, three days."

"Is there a trail?" George asked.

"No trail—go in forest."

"Could you show us the way? Be our guide? I would pay you," George said, anxious to save any time.

"Yes. Yes. I go with you."

"Then it is settled. When can you be ready to go?"

"Now. Get gun, food from house." The man disappeared toward the village.

George noticed Gist looked worried. "What is it, Mr. Gist? You do not seem pleased at our good fortune in finding this guide. He will show us the shortest route and we will save time."

"I am almost sure I saw this Indian at Joncaire's," Gist said.

"I do not remember seeing him at all." George brushed Gist's concerns aside.

The man soon reappeared dressed for travel. "I carry pack for you, Conotocarious," he offered.

"Thank you," George said, slipping the burdensome thing off his back. The three men quickly left Murdering Town behind them. They traveled briskly for eight or ten miles. But as twilight came, George began to lag behind.

Gist asked, "Is there anything the matter, Major?"

George hated to admit it. "My feet are sore and I am weary. It is as you said would happen. I am exhausted." He half apologized for his insulting outburst to Gist the day before. "I think we should camp."

On hearing this, the Indian offered, "I carry your gun. It is heavy."

"You are carrying two packs and your own gun now. That is enough."

"I offer help. You not trust me?" he asked crossly.

"It is better if we each carry our own gun," George insisted. But the man's attitude caused him a little concern. He was not about to give him two guns. Besides, he did not intend to go a step farther. He sat down on a log. "Make a fire and let us eat. I am starving."

"No!" the Indian said. "We go."

"We want to camp here," Gist insisted.

"French Ottawas in woods. We go to my cabin. Be safe there," he warned.

"How far to your cabin?" Gist asked.

"Hear gun to my cabin."

The Indian did not wait for Gist and George. He started off again.

"I think he is leading us too far in a north-easterly direction," Gist whispered to George. "We should be going southeast to get to the Allegheny."

"If we could get to a cabin tonight, I would be so grateful," George said, ignoring Gist's warning again.

"Very well," Gist said reluctantly.

They walked about two miles more, veering left toward the north instead of right toward the south. Gist stopped. "How far now?"

"Hear two whoops."

Again they walked, but no cabin loomed up out of the darkness.

Finally, George gave up any thought of a cabin. He could not go another step. "We will stop at the next creek and wait for morning," he ordered the man, who was fifteen or twenty paces ahead of him.

The Indian made no reply and kept walking. They broke out of the trees and began to cross a meadow. It was quite light because of the snow on the ground. They could see where they were going for once instead of stumbling among the thickets of the deep forest. George thought this would be a good place to stop. He called, "Find water. We will stop here."

Suddenly, the Indian turned, bringing his gun up as he did. He took dead aim at Gist and George and fired.

"Are you shot?" George asked.

"No!" Gist answered.

The Indian ran ahead and crouched behind a big oak tree in the middle of the meadow to reload his gun. George and Gist ran after him. George made a flying leap and knocked the gun from his hands. Over and over they rolled in the snow as the man tried every trick to loosen George's grip on him. But George had made himself into an expert wrestler in his childhood, and he soon had the Indian pinned to the ground.

Gist drew his scalping knife and raised it for the kill.

"NO!" George gasped when he saw Gist was bent on murder.

Gist stared at George in utter disbelief. "Are you so much the gentleman you shrink from death even to defend yourself?"

George ignored him. He let the man up as he said reasonably, "You frightened us by using your gun like that." But George did not return the gun to the Indian. He held it as well as his own. "Let us find a stream and make camp," he said as if nothing unusual had happened except a little accident.

The three men continued to walk across the meadow with the Indian leading the way. Once in the trees again, they found a small frozen creek. "We will stop here. Make a fire," George ordered.

The Indian collected dry sticks and soon had a small fire burning. George set about making camp. Gist followed his example, not knowing what he was about. But George always stayed near the guns leaning against a tree and Gist never took his eyes off the Indian.

"Major," Gist whispered, "As you will not have him killed, we must get him away and then we must travel all night."

"Yes. That is what we must do, but how?"

"Let me." Gist went to the Indian who was working on the fire. "I suppose you were lost and fired your gun," he said pleasantly.

"I know trail to cabin now. It little way," the frightened man answered.

"Well, you go home and as we are much tired, we will follow your track in the morning." Gist opened his pack and rummaged around inside. Finally, he pulled out some food. "Here is a cake of bread for you, and you must give us meat in the morning," he ordered.

"Yes, yes, you come morning. I have food ready." The man scrambled to his feet and ran off into the trees, thankful his life had been spared for some reason by the Englishmen.

Silently, Gist followed him at a distance and

then stopped to listen as the breaking of sticks told him the Indian continued to make his way through the forest away from the camp.

Satisfied at last he was not doubling back, Gist returned to the campfire. "Let's go!"

George started to kick snow on the fire.

"Let it burn. Anyone approaching will think we are still here."

Picking up their packs and guns, they retreated into the woods in the opposite direction the Indian had taken.

Chapter Ten

The Raft and the River

Thursday, December 27, 1753—The Wilderness

Goaded by danger, George sprinted through the woods on Gist's heels. They ran half a mile before they stopped and listened a long, long time. "Get out some paper, George. We need to make a fire quickly."

"I think we need to travel many more miles before we consider camping."

"We have to know where we are going. Do you want to go in circles and meet our so-called guide again, maybe with some of his friends this time?" Gist asked impatiently. "I am sure now he was lying in wait for us at Murdering Town. I thought I saw him at Joncaire's. You can wager he is not ready to give up yet. Come daylight, he will easily track us in the snow. Fortunately, winter nights are long. If we are lucky, we will have time to get beyond his reach by morning."

George pulled some blank sheets of paper from his pack. Striking his flint, Gist soon made them into a torch. Quickly, he set his compass and fixed a course southeast for the Allegheny River. In the last flickering light Christopher Gist looked up and studied George's face. "If we are to have any chance to get away from the French Indians, we will have to travel without stopping all night. Are you able?"

"I am able," George answered. There was no choice. Either keep up or die.

Gist scattered the ashes into the wind. Each man secured his pack to his back, pulled his matchcoat close around himself, and checked his gun to make sure it was in firing order.

They tramped all night. In the morning, they reached the head of a creek where they stopped to eat come corn cakes from their packs and break the ice for water. The danger of death had kept George's blood up through the night. But now his energy was gone. The small amount of cold food did little to restore him. But he made no complaint.

Christopher Gist checked his compass again. "We will follow this creek. It goes in a general southeast direction and, I believe, will empty into the Allegheny River."

George's iron will forced him to stand, pick up his heavy gun, and start the forced march again. If Gist could travel night and day, George was determined he could, too. Had he not bragged, cruelly, that his youth made him more able? "What a bad tasting stew one's own words make to eat," he thought.

"I wish it would snow," Gist said when they were able to walk side by side.

"Do we not have enough hardships?"

"If it snowed, our tracks would be covered and the air would be warmer," Gist reminded him.

It was almost night again when suddenly Gist stopped. "Oh no!" He crouched down close to the ground to examine it. "See these tracks? Indians have been here today."

Fear struck George so hard he began to tremble. "Our guide and his friends?"

Gist studied the ground all around. "I think it was a hunting party."

"What tribe?" George asked, still remembering the Ottawas.

"I don't know, but we must separate and leave two different trails. It will confuse them. I will cross the creek. You stay on this side. I know now this is Piney Creek. There is a big rock downstream. We will meet there."

"But it is almost dark. How will I find my way? I am not an Indian with night vision," George protested, remembering the messenger from Nathaniel Gist. His words covered his real fear of being totally alone in the forest with French Indians about.

"Keep near the creek," Gist said impatiently. "We must be off. The Indians may have crossed here and gone on, or they still may be around."

Reluctantly, George parted from Gist, who crossed the creek and was soon lost from sight in the trees. His heart pounded and his legs trembled as he walked rapidly or ran, where possible, along the bank of the frozen stream. He stopped to listen. Were those cracking sounds such as the man had made running from the camp? No, it must be the winter wind in the tree-tops. George started again. At an opening in the thicket, he forced himself away from the creek to make a confusing trail. But the creek was frozen and there was no sound of rushing water to tell him where it was in the darkness. He returned to it quickly.

Mile after mile he walked—ran—stopped—listened. Thoughts of death forced their way into his mind. What would an arrow in his back feel like, or a tomahawk in his skull? If he were captured alive, would Tanacharison save him from an unspeakable death? His heart leaped irregularly in his chest when his footfall disturbed an animal and sent it scampering.

Where was the rock? On and on George ran, tripping over bare tree roots, slipping on icy rocks. Maybe Gist was wrong. Maybe this was not Piney Creek and there was no rock. All these creeks looked alike. Had he not crossed hundreds of them in the last two months? Panic seized him again. He fought it down and tried to think rationally. "This stream must empty into the Allegheny River. I will keep on until I get there. Then I can find my way to Frazier's. There is a way out of this." He concentrated on his plan. So deep was he in thought that he did not see the huge outcropping of stone until he stumbled into it.

Gratefully, he leaned against the rock and put his arms out as if to embrace it. Then he slid down to the ground and leaned his back to it. When Gist reached the rock later in the night, he found Major George Washington sound asleep.

The sunlight flickering on his eyelids awoke George. It took him only seconds to realize he had placed himself in great danger by foolishly falling asleep. He jumped up and stumbled over the body of Christopher Gist curled up on the ground. "Christopher? Oh thank God you are here. Are you all right?"

"Well, I was until I was awakened with a kick."

"Do you think we are safe?"

"No, but let us eat and then be on our way again. The Allegheny is not much farther. Once we walk across the river on the ice, we should be safe. Tonight we will be at Frazier's, God willing."

"Hallelujah!" George exclaimed at the thought of a warm cabin, a warm bed, warm food.

They made a small fire, melted snow, and made tea. "I wish we had some of St. Pierre's brandy to lace this tea," George sighed.

They heated dried meat over the fire and hastily gulped corn cakes, washing them down with tea. Then they struck out again following

Piney Creek. Within two hours, they heard the roar of rushing water. Gist stopped. "That must be the Allegheny."

"It must be. At last!" George started to run headlong through the trees, but he stopped short. "Oh no, NO!" He buried his face in his hands.

Gist trudged up behind him and put a hand on his shoulder. "We should not be able to hear it," he said quietly.

Fifty yards out from the near and far banks there were thick sheets of ice. But in the center of the quarter-mile-wide river was violent white water.

The two men watched the river for a long time in silence. George spoke first. "We must cross it, Christopher. We cannot spend the winter on this side. Do you think we might find an abandoned canoe along the river?"

"Even if we were so fortunate, a frail canoe could never withstand the pounding of those ice flows," Gist said practically.

"Then we must make a raft," George said.

"A raft? How?"

"My brothers and I used to make rafts and float them in the little creeks on our farm—if Mother did not catch us. I have a hatchet. I will start to fell small trees. You take your knife and peel strips of bark to tie the logs together."

"But we could never build something that would hold us and make it across that wild river," Gist argued.

"Do you have a better idea?" George asked. But then he said quickly, "It is my fault we are in this bad spot. I can find my way from here, Christopher. I do not need a guide. I am discharging you. You can follow the river down to the forks and then to Logstown and spend the winter there in Croghan's storehouse. Monacatoocha will welcome you even if Tanacharison stays in Venango."

"Let us both go to Logstown. The Indians will help us cross the river. The Ohio is quieter than this Allegheny," Gist said.

But George had already thought of going to Logstown and discarded the idea. "It would take us three or four more days to go down to Logstown and then three or four more to come up on the other side. And we would be on the wrong side of the Monongahela from Frazier's. His place is ten miles from here once we get across the river. I will not go fifty or a hundred miles out of my way."

He began hacking at a nearby young tree. With only one hatchet between them, they took turns at the backbreaking work. Weakened by the cold, night and day travel, and little food, their progress was slow. George finally said, "I'll chop. You shoot some game. We might as well eat while we are stopped."

The work went on all day. Just after sunset, they tied the last log and straightened up. "Now we will push it down the bank and across the ice shelf and launch it."

"We had better wait for morning," Gist said.

"There are Indians in these woods. Let us be away from here," George insisted.

They tied their packs and guns to the little platform. Then they pushed it toward open water across the ice. Easing the raft into the river, George held the bobbing platform while Gist with two long setting poles in his hand boarded. Then George jumped on. "Push off!" he ordered as they dug their long poles into the river bottom and edged the raft out into the main stream. One yard, two yards, three yards into the river they guided their craft. Gist was on the upstream side, George, the downstream. But soon the current took hold and tossed the little raft around like an empty eggshell despite the combined strength of the two powerful men to control it.

Somehow, they were able to get halfway across the river when the raft became wedged in an ice jam coming downriver. It crunched against the platform and tilted it. "We must hold it until the ice passes," George yelled. He jammed his long pole down to the bottom of the river, holding it at a sharp angle toward him and bracing his shoulder against it. But his strength was as nothing against the raging river. The combined current and ice threw the raft against the pole and pushed it forward violently. George was flipped into the Allegheny.

Instantly, he was almost paralyzed by the

freezing water as he was swept along in the swift current. He tried to yell for help, but the water choked off his cries. The raft was upon him.

Abandoning his setting pole, Gist tried to grasp George, but failed. "Grab the raft!" he yelled. George reached up to fend off the raft that was bent on pushing his head under. He caught hold of a rough log and somehow held on. Gist grabbed him by his matchcoat and pulled. "Got you," he called. Little by little, George inched his way back on top of the raft as it was tossed and twisted by the will of the river. He lay on the logs gasping for breath. Then he pulled himself up with Gist's help and the two men using one setting pole tried to control the raft again. Mighty was the struggle between the men and the river, but the river won.

Just then the raft swept close by an island. Without a word spoken between them, Christopher and George knew what they had to do. Quickly, they untied their packs and guns from the raft and jumped into the river. They waded ashore and threw themselves down on the sand.

When Gist had caught his breath, he called to George, "Are you all right?" There was no reply. Christopher Gist dragged himself over to where George lay sprawled on the sand and shook him. "George? George! Answer me!"

"Huh." George uttered a sound.

"You can't go to sleep!" Gist yelled.

George did not move.

"Get up, George, get up!" Gist got to his knees and began pulling at him.

"I'm so tired," George mumbled.

"Get up. You'll freeze to death. We've got to make a fire."

Gist let George go for a moment. He crawled on his hands and knees looking for something to burn. There was nothing. No driftwood. Not a stick. Not a dry leaf.

Christopher Gist went back to George and dragged him roughly to his feet.

"No!" George protested, "I've got to sleep. I'll die if I don't sleep." But he was too exhausted to fight Gist off.

"You'll die if you do!" Gist pulled one of George's long arms around his own shoulders. As he grasped George's hand, he saw it was torn and bleeding from the log on the raft. There was nothing he could do. The blood would freeze and stop.

The two men dragged themselves around and around the tiny island. They found no trees, no rocks, no shelter of any kind. The wind howled down the river, colder and colder each hour.

"Keep walking, George, we must keep walking," Christopher said over and over through the frigid December night. But before the long night ended, it was George who carried Christopher.

"George, I fear my fingers and toes are frostbitten," Gist said, dropping down on the sand.

"We cannot give up now, Christopher. It will be morning soon."

"And then what? How are we to get to either shore? Have you forgotten we are on an island? We must cross more deep water before we can get to the north bank."

"I will swim across, get to Frazier's, and come back for you." George explained the plan he had decided on during the night.

"In that current, amidst the ice flow? You are mad," Gist dismissed the plan disgustedly.

"If I survived that dunking I took last night, I can probably make it. We will take stock of our situation at first light. Our survival of this night is our first problem. I will try to warm your feet." George began to unlace Gist's moccasins. But he could hardly bend down for the wet leather of his leggings, moccasins, and matchcoat had frozen stiff.

When the gray dawn finally came, George said with a strange cheerfulness, "Well, I'll be, we are still alive. At least the weather is bound to get warmer with daylight."

"If you say so, George." Gist could not help but smile at the high hopes of youth.

"Guess I will go look at the river." Stiffly, George got up on all fours and then forced himself into a standing position. He looked around. "I do not believe my eyes!" he yelled. He started off, limping, as fast as he could toward the north side of the island.

Gist pulled himself into a sitting position and watched as George reached the river and gingerly began to walk upon it. Then he turned around and ran in a crazy lope back toward Gist. "It is shut up hard, Christopher, all the way to the shore. It will support us both."

"God be praised!"

"Amen!" George shouted, throwing his arms up to the sky. "Let us get to shore immediately. There is wood there. We will build a great fire, dry out our clothes, warm your hands and feet, and eat! Take hold of me, Christopher. Get up slowly."

Painfully, the older man got to his feet. George put both packs on his own back. "Christopher, can you carry your gun?"

"Yes, I think so," Gist replied, his face reflecting the awful pain in his hands as he tried to bend them around his gun.

"All right, lean on me until we get to the shore." George half carried, half dragged Gist to the riverbank. Once there, Gist sat down and studied the ice himself.

"See?" George said. "It is strong."

Gist nodded again. "You go ahead, George. Take the packs and the guns to the other side."

"Then I'll come back for you," George said.

"No. The ice with only one night of freezing will not hold both of our weights in one place."

"I am not leaving you here, Christopher.

Either we both get over or we both go in."

"I'll get on my own," Gist insisted. "Go ahead of me and test the ice."

George started. Ten feet, twenty-five feet, fifty feet out onto the ice. Then he looked back at Christopher Gist. He was slowly, steadily coming—on his hands and knees.

George reached the bank and climbed up. As Gist crawled across the ice, George got out his flint, gathered leaves and sticks, and made a fire. When it was flaming steadily, he went back down the bank and helped push and pull Gist up. The older man collapsed before the fire.

George fed the flames until they were roaring. They stripped off their frozen clothes and dried them. Gist gently massaged his toes and fingers near the heat while taking sips of strong tea.

By noon, they were much restored. "Well, George, are you ready to go?"

"You mean you wish to start for Frazier's? With your frostbite, I think we should stay here tonight."

"If we walked across the ice, the Ottawas can, too. I want to get to Frazier's," Gist insisted.

They made their way across the ten miles of land between the Allegheny and Monongahela Rivers. Gist had to walk slowly and George limped a little. Both fashioned stout walking sticks to lean on.

As the afternoon wore on, George kept

sniffing the air for the telltale signs of smoke that meant they were near Frazier's. It was after dark before George caught the drift. If he had not had to wait for Gist and help him walk, he would have run the rest of the way to Frazier's. What had once been a tiny, humble log hut to George now loomed in his mind as great as any palace. But the two men were forced to approach their goal at the same slow pace.

George kept taking deep, reassuring breaths. Suddenly, he stopped. "Christopher, I think I smell too much smoke, don't you?"

Gist, who had been forced to concentrate completely on each step he walked, had taken little notice of the smoke. Now he took a deep breath, then another. "You're right."

George had been carrying Gist's gun as well as his own. But now he handed one gun to Gist. "I will go ahead and scout," he whispered. "You stay here." George dropped the packs off his back. His moccasins made no sound as he slipped through the forest, crouching low in the thickets and hiding behind the huge trees.

Gist moved the packs off the trail and hid himself behind some bushes to await George's return.

The minutes dragged by one by one until half an hour had passed before George came back. "Christopher, where are you?"

Gist scrambled back to the trail where George was searching for him. With their heads close, George whispered, "There is a war party camped all around Frazier's."

Chapter Eleven

The War Party

Sunday, December 30, 1753—Turtle Creek

Christopher Gist closed his eyes. Both men had prodded and pushed themselves to the limit of their endurance and beyond by sheer force of their wills to reach the safety of John Frazier's cabin. It was the dream that kept them struggling one mile more, one mile more. Now they were within sight of their goal and it was denied to them.

"What are they?" Gist asked in a dull voice, no longer caring. "How many?"

"About twenty. I think Iroquois, but I cannot be sure." George tried to put the best light on their desperate situation. "Once when I was at Colonel Cresap's trading post, an Iroquois war party came back up the Warrior's Path after attacking the Cherokees. But they meant no harm to the Englishmen. They were friends of Cresap's."

Gist took no notice of George's words. "We will have to make a wide circle around them through the woods."

But George knew Christopher would never be able to make it. "You are frozen. You cannot stay out in the open another night."

"What choice do I have?"

"I am a brother to the Iroquois now," George said.

"This war party may not have been told of your new status," Gist said sarcastically. "And these fellows may not be Iroquois."

"I only went to this side of Turtle Creek. It is safe that far, I think," George said.

"All right. Let's go have a look." Gist struggled to his feet.

George picked up the two packs, but each man carried his own gun. Noiselessly, they made their way along the trail to Turtle Creek. They crawled behind a thicket on the bank and looked toward Frazier's cabin. Thin smoke came from the chimney. In the clearing several fires burned. Warriors crouched around them cooking and eating.

Gist watched for a long time. "They are Iroquois all right, but I see no sign of Frazier."

"He may need help," George said. "We have guns."

"So do they." Gist pointed out guns leaning against trees.

"We are dressed as Indians. With our faces hidden, we could probably walk through the camp to Frazier's cabin and not be noticed."

They watched silently again for a long time. Finally, George said, "We will freeze if we stay here much longer." For another winter night was upon them. "Either we must circle around or we must go into the camp. Frazier has lived among these people for years. I do not think they would harm him." George stated what he hoped was a fact.

"You are counting on his protection? Have you forgotten that eleven white traders including George Croghan could not save a white woman?" Gist reminded George.

"Can you travel ten, twenty miles by morning and keep on traveling?" George asked. "Are you able?"

"No," Gist admitted. "But you are. Get away while you can. You must get back to Williamsburg."

"As I said on the island, Christopher, we either both get across or we both go in. We will wait here and watch until the camp sleeps. Then we will go in and hope they do not notice us."

Gist began feeling around on the ground and bushes near him. At last he came up with some dirt and berries. "Here, George, rub this on your face. It will help to hide your whiteness."

As they waited, one by one the Indians rolled up in their fur robes and went to sleep by the fires. Slowly, the flames died to embers and the encampment was almost dark.

"I do not think they have posted guards," Gist said. "They usually don't unless they know enemies are near."

"Why a war party? Tanacharison said his

people don't make war in winter," George asked.

"Tanacharison is wise and cares for his people. This chief may think differently. Perhaps somebody raided them and they are out for revenge. Who knows?"

"Do you think the time is right, Christopher?" George was trembling with cold from sitting still hours in the snow.

"Are you sure you want to do this?" Gist asked again.

"I think we are committed. If we were to run for it, we should have gone hours ago."

George and Gist crawled back to the trail. They stood up and fastened their packs once again to their backs. They pulled their coats up around their heads to hide their faces. George held his gun ready. Gist put his knife in the front of his belt.

Like huge shadows, they cautiously crept across frozen Turtle Creek. The deep snow muffled their steps, but also hid the treacherous roots and rocks as they picked their way across the open ground toward Frazier's cabin. Their effort was small, but their breath came fast and hard. George feared the loud pounding of his heart surely would wake the warriors as they crept past them.

Once the familiar rough-hewn door was before them, Gist hesitated. He looked at George. But George did not wait. He kicked the door open. A gun blasted.

George threw himself down on the dirt floor.

"Frazier! It's Gist!"

"Oh my God!" cried the familiar gravelly voice. "Are you shot?" Frazier pushed the door shut for the whole camp of warriors was up and heading for it. "Who's with you?" he asked, leveling his gun at George crumpled up on the floor.

"George Washington," Gist yelled.

"Get your guns at the slots. I'll try to calm the men down," Frazier ordered. "Hodenosaunees! It is all right. I had an accident fixing a gun," he said in their language through the door. "Go back to sleep."

The Indians milled around the cabin. George tensely held his gun in a firing slot but kept it from showing through on the outside. Gist did the same on another wall. Frazier remained by the door talking.

"What are they doing here?" Gist asked in a low voice when the Indians finally returned to their campfires. "Is there an uprising?"

"Do ya think my cabin would be standing if there was?"

"You fix their guns, John. You are more useful to them alive than dead," Gist said.

"I don't never count on that. This bunch told me they was goin' south t' make war on the Cherokees. But they come t' a cabin at the head o' the Great Kanawha River and found men n' women n' children killed n' scalped, seven in all. They said the people were lyin' about the house n' the bodies was torn up and eaten by wild hogs."

"Who were they? Got any idea, John?"

"There's a settlement down that way, but these poor folks musta been out a ways. Anyway, these Iroquois forgot about the Cherokees and got outta there. Said they didn't want the English thinkin' they done it and rise up against their towns."

"Do these Indians have any idea who did the killings?" Gist asked.

"Said from the marks, the French Ottawas done it."

George and Christopher exchanged a look.

Frazier went on. "Strange thing, though. The Iroquois said one woman killed had long, blond hair. The Ottawas didn't take her scalp."

Frazier put down his gun at last and built up the fire. He put some meat on the spit and patted out some corn cakes, dropping them in the spider pan where they floated in sputtering bear grease.

George and Gist took off their matchcoats and stood by the fire warming themselves. When Frazier finally put the food on the table, the two exhausted men ate everything before them. Frazier set out tin mugs and poured cider from a stone jug. "You sleep, I'll stand guard."

"Christopher, you take the bed," George said.

Gist did not argue that his superior should have the best accommodations. Frazier helped George pile some shaggy buffalo robes on the dirt floor before the fire. George crawled into the robes and within minutes was fast asleep, his outstretched hand on his gun.

George was awakened by the sound of low voices. "He's a brave lad, John. In fact, he has too much courage for his own good sometimes."

"Well, didn't we all when we was his age."

"Loyal, too. He could have gotten away last night through the woods when he saw the war party. But he wouldn't leave me and he was worried about you."

"Sign o' a good commander," Frazier remarked. "Loyalty to his men."

George could not allow this conversation to continue without making his presence known. He started to stir within the nest of buffalo robes.

"Mornin', Major," Frazier greeted him, raising his mug of steaming tea in salute.

George sat up stiffly. "The Indians?"

"They're gone. Left this mornin'."

"The rest of our expedition is coming up from Logstown in a week or two. Can they expect trouble from this war party or the Ottawas?" George asked anxiously, thinking of the inexperienced Van Braam.

"Used to be winter was pretty safe. The Indians stayed in their lodges. But these are troubled times n' they are restless. Better the rest come ahead now than wait in Logstown till spring and the French stir up trouble."

Again Gist and George exchanged looks. Then George told Frazier of the trouble the French planned for spring. "So you see, Mr. Frazier, I must get back to Williamsburg as fast as possible. Do you have horses I could purchase? For travel by foot will be too slow."

"I'll go around t' the Indian village n' see if they be willin' t' trade." Frazier went to the pegs in the logs and took down a fur coat. "You stay here."

George pulled the greatly deflated money pouch from around his neck. "Here is money," he offered.

"Indians don't want coins. I'll trade 'em somethin'. Jest hope they got horses and ain't eaten 'em yet."

"Oh, I guess I better tell ya," he said, pausing at the door of the cabin. "Queen Alliquippa was by here n' is real insulted that you didn't pay a call on her when you was here on the way out."

"Who is Queen Alli . . . ?" George asked, very puzzled.

"She's head woman of a Seneca clan who rules a tribe of Delawares near here," Gist said.

"A *woman* chief?" George asked disbelievingly.

"Yes, and a very important one, too," Frazier answered.

"Think I should pay a social call?" George asked, hoping Frazier would advise against it. He did not want to go out in the cold again.

"The English need every Indian friend they can get, and right now she is a great friend of the English."

"All right. But I have no presents."

"I got some rum in the chest there," Frazier said. "Take a bottle and there is an extra matchcoat I got in trade."

"Thank you, Mr. Frazier."

George and Gist ate breakfast, left the cabin, and walked three miles to the mouth of the Youghiogheny River. When they entered the village of Queen Alliquippa, they had to make themselves understood by a few words and much sign language. Finally, they were ushered into a smoky wigwam and the presence of the queen.

When his eyes became accustomed to the dim light, George saw a middle-aged woman sitting on a buffalo robe before the fire stirring the contents of a kettle. She looked at George sternly, then pointed at him.

Gist did his best through a mixture of Indian and English words and much pointing to learn the wishes of the queen. At last he said, "The queen does not think you are important. You look like a long trader, not a messenger from the great King across the water. She expected the uniform she heard the King's men wear. She is much displeased."

George choked back a laugh the best he could. He pulled back the hood of his coat. His brown hair was no longer caught in a neat queue at the back of his neck, but flowed out in a tangled mat about his shoulders. His face was still covered with dirt and red berry juice. But he swept an elaborate bow to the queen and then he displayed the matchcoat before her with as much flair as he could muster.

Alliquippa paid little attention to it until George laid the bottle of rum atop the gift of the coat. The queen grabbed the bottle up and held it to her. Now she smiled broadly, indicating George and Gist were to sit on the buffalo robe. She began ladling stew out of the kettle into clay dishes for them. George Washington and Christopher Gist spent the last day of 1753 dining with a queen.

It was almost dark as they made their way back to Frazier's. A beautiful sight awaited them; before Frazier's cabin stood two horses.

"They were the best I could do," Frazier apologized.

George, an expert horseman, looked them over. They were far from sleek, but they looked strong of limb and sound of wind. They were better than walking.

George and Christopher traveled another week back over the mountains, across frozen streams and rivers. With two strong horses and no baggage, they traveled faster. But neither did they have a tent to give them even minimal shelter at night. They found cabins, fashioned lean-tos, or looked for caves, but several mornings they awoke to find themselves buried in snow.

At last, on January 7, they spent the night comfortably at Gist's settlement on Will's Creek. Gist urged George to stay and rest up for he had at least another week of wilderness travel—alone—to reach Williamsburg.

But George would not be persuaded and Gist understood him by now. On their last morning in each other's company, Gist stood very straight and saluted. "Major, it would be an honor to serve under you any time. You lead a charmed life to have escaped injury or even death in all your daring."

Now that he was to take his leave, George did not know how to put his deep feelings into the right words. He was angry at his failure to be able to express himself, so he reverted to the safety of stiff formality. He looked at Gist gravely. "It was I who served a wilderness apprenticeship under you. You may be sure Governor Dinwiddie will hear about your great service and devotion to the completion of this mission." George cursed himself silently. Devotion! What a poor word. This man had saved his life, saved the expedition, saved the Indian alliance.

Gist looked down at the floor a moment as he struggled to suppress a smile at young

George's clumsy attempts to say thank you. "Farewell, Conotocarious." He held out his hand.

George grasped it. "Until we meet again—Annosanah." They both knew the ordeals they had shared would bind them in deep friendship forever. Nothing more needed to be said.

George wrapped himself in his matchcoat and mounted his horse. He did not look back, not until he reached the stream. "Aguyase!" he called, and raised his arm in salute to Gist.

Chapter Twelve

"And the King Shall Know Your Name"

Wednesday, January 16, 1754—Williamsburg, Colony and Dominion of Virginia

George Washington returned to Williamsburg exactly one month after he had pushed off in the canoe from Fort Le Boeuf. For that month, he had been on the trail, on foot, or on horseback, every day except two—New Year's Eve at John Frazier's and January 11 when he had stopped at Belvoir, the home of Colonel Fairfax. There he had two nights' sleep in a feather bed and a day of rest. He ate fine food off china plates with silver utensils. He had a bath. He caught his hair back in a queue again and exchanged his Indian dress for the clothes of a gentleman. But in his heart part of him would always be Conotocarious. He knew he would return to the wilderness as Christopher Gist did. To its incredible dangers, its loneliness, its tests of total self-reliance. To Tanacharison who believed he could become a great warrior and chief to the English people as his years increased. For he had survived, and therefore he was set apart from other men forever.

Major George Washington, Esquire, adjutant for the southern district, rode into Williamsburg to find the town quiet. A soft blanket of snow lay on the ground. People stayed close to their hearths. Christmas was over. The House of Burgesses and the courts would not meet again until Publick Times in April. How it had changed since he left when the days were warm, the trees red and gold, and the town crowded with people for October Publick Times. He had experienced so much, George felt he had been gone far longer than one change of seasons. He rode up the green under the bare catalpa trees until he saw the red brick wall of the Palace where Governor Robert Dinwiddie lived.

George halted and dismounted at the front gate in the serpentine brick wall that set off the Palace from the rest of the town. A young footman ran out to take the reins of his horse. "Who may I say is calling, Sir?" he asked.

"Major George Washington."

The footman blinked, then blinked again as if George were some sort of apparition—indeed, a ghost. "Mr. Smythe! Mr. Smythe!" he called loudly, never taking his eyes off George.

An older man ran out of the front door of the Palace. He wore no cloak against the January winds. The young footman was so excited he could hardly speak.

"Sir, this gentleman claims to be Major

George Washington, but Major Washington is dead!"

George roared with laughter at the absurd situation. "Mr. Smythe, be not afraid. I am indeed no ghost," he reassured the Governor's butler, whom he had met before on visits to the Palace.

The butler looked at George. "Heaven be praised, it IS Major Washington. Major Washington has returned!" His shouts brought workers rushing to the courtyard.

Governor Dinwiddie was peering out of the window of his office to see what all the excitement was about when his secretary, William Withers, burst in. "Your Honour, your Honour . . . Ma, Ma . . ." Withers was so excited he could not get the words out. He tried again. "Major Washington has returned! He is here!"

Governor Dinwiddie rushed from his office as fast as his years and his bulk would allow him. He was halfway down the passage in the center of the Palace when he saw George standing in the doorway. "Major Washington—welcome. We have long awaited your arrival!"

George saluted.

Governor Dinwiddie led the way back to his office, which also served as his dining room. The governor collapsed into an armchair, breathing heavily from his excitement. He motioned George to take another chair close to the fire.

Before he sat down, George reached into

his pocket and pulled out the sealed letter wrapped in oilcloth and handed it to Governor Dinwiddie. "The reply of the French commander in the Ohio, Jacques Legardeur, Sieur de Saint Pierre, to your letter, your Honour."

"St. Pierre?" Dinwiddie raised his eyebrow. "I had heard the name de Marin."

"De Marin is dead, Sir."

"Oh. Well, I know you have much to tell me."

"Indeed I have, Sir."

Dinwiddie broke the seal on the letter from the French and proceeded to read it.

George could see the writing was as crisp as the day it had been penned. The icy waters of the Allegheny River never reached it.

The Governor read silently, nodding his head from time to time or snorting in disgust. Finally, he looked up at George with an expression of grim delight on his face. "Well, it is as I have said all along. The French claim the Ohio territory and contest the pretensions—pretensions indeed!—of the King of Great Britain to it. This St. Pierre seems to imply they will back up their claim with force, if necessary."

"Indeed they will, Sir," George started to reply.

But Dinwiddie interrupted him. "I held the Council and the Burgesses in session until December 19, Major. I wish I had had this letter to lay before them, proof of my suspicions that

Virginia's frontiers need protection."

George felt a hint of faultfinding from Dinwiddie that he had not returned sooner. "It was not possible, Sir. I was five hundred miles from Williamsburg. Indeed, I was but a few miles from the south shore of Lake Erie itself on December 19."

Governor Dinwiddie's sunken eyes opened wide. "You had to go as far as Lake Erie to present my letter?"

"Yes, Sir. And the route could not be direct, so I traveled much more than a thousand miles on my journey." He leaned forward. "Sir, the French plan more than to defend themselves. They plan a massive offensive in the spring. At Fort Le Boeuf, they were building hundreds of canoes. I met French army deserters who had come up from New Orleans on the Mississippi River, the River Ohio, and a river called the Obaish . . ."

"What?" Dinwiddie almost bolted from his chair. "Major, start at the beginning. Don't leave anything out."

George pulled his notes from his pocket. Some were not easy to read considering the circumstances they had been written under. But he began and took Governor Robert Dinwiddie along on his strange journey.

He talked for hours; Dinwiddie interrupted with questions. As he finished his report, George added one thing. "I recommend to you, Sir, and the Council the services of Christopher Gist. The Dominion of Virginia and I, personally, owe him a debt we can never repay for the completion of this mission. I also wish to recommend John Davison who acted as my interpreter to the Indians and did a most splendid job, as did the traders Barnaby Currin, John MacQuire, Henry Steward, and William Jenkins. And one other, Sir, a Dutch gentleman named Jacob Van Braam who was my interpreter to the French. He is a trained army officer and we might need his services someday. One more most important report, your Honour. Tanacharison, the Half King, remains our brother. He is a great man." With these words, George Washington felt he had completed the mission given to him by the Governor and the Council.

"Major Washington, I personally thank you. Your mission was a great success, a great success. We are grateful to the Almighty that you came through such trials as you have described safe and sound."

George was puzzled. "But Your Honour, the French are not willing to leave the Ohio," he protested.

"I did not expect they would." Then he leaned forward and almost whispered to George. "I had orders signed by his most gracious majesty, King George himself, to inquire into the truth of whether any number of persons whether Indians or Europeans presumed to erect any fort within the limits of our province of Virginia. I was first to require them to peaceably depart. And if they still carried on such designs, I am charged and commanded to drive them out by force! You, George Washington, have carried out the orders of the King himself! I sent the letter telling the French to leave His Majesty's lands. They have replied they will not. With your own eyes you have seen at least one newly built fort and been told about others. Between the letter and your eyewitness account, I can now use force. You bravely went forward when others turned back in fear. Believe me, Major Washington, the King himself will hear your name and the service you have given him. I will send a letter by the first ship."

George dared not smile, but he was pleased beyond his wildest dreams. He had served his King! Not the Ohio Company.

Governor Dinwiddie went on. "When you did not return, I ordered William Trent to go to the Forks of the Ohio and build a fort."

"Yes, Christopher Gist and I met Trent and his men on the trail as we returned. The bare triangle of land at the Forks is an ideal place to build a fort. It will command the Allegheny and Monongahela Rivers as well as the River Ohio. Allow me to show you on my map."

Dinwiddie studied the map again. "I have another request, indeed, I'm afraid I must order you to write an account of your journey. The

Council meets tomorrow and I want them to know all you have learned. Show them I have been right all along. Maybe now I can get the House of Burgesses to vote the funds we need to raise an army."

"By tomorrow, Sir?"

"Yes, yes. I must have it by tomorrow. I know you can do it. Now, you have much to do—and so do I. I dismiss you, Major. Go along and write of your journey and return tomorrow morning."

George rose from his chair and saluted. One day to write up two and a half months. He knew he was not a skilled writer because of his lack of education. But he could not protest; he was under orders.

He left the Governor's office. Outside in the courtyard of the Palace workers still stood about. When they saw him, they cheered. The footmen scrambled for the honor of bringing him his horse. He nodded to them, then mounted up. Riding back along the Palace green, he hoped Mr. Wetherburn would have a private room at his tavern with a large supply of candles.

George wrote the rest of the day and through the night. In the end he wrote about seven thousand words. He was not satisfied with it, but he had no time to revise his work. It was the best he could do in the short time given to him.

"I hope it will be sufficient to satisfy your

Honour with my Proceedings; for that was my Aim in undertaking the Journey, and chief Study throughout the Prosecution of it.

"With the Hope of doing it, I, with infinite Pleasure, subscribe myself,

> Your Honour's most Obedient,
> And very humble Servant,
>
> G. Washington"

Epilogue

When Washington turned the journal over to Governor Dinwiddie the next day, the Governor was delighted. Immediately, he sent for William Hunter of Williamsburg to print up copies. He intended to give them to important men in Virginia and send them to the governors of the other colonies and to London to alert them of the true danger from the French.

George was horrified to learn his hurried efforts at writing this story of his mission would be printed and seen by others. He insisted on penning a message of apology to be printed with it.

The people of Williamsburg eagerly read his amazing journal. Some were thrilled by his adventure, and some considered it merely a tall tale. Whether it was cheered or jeered, the journal made George Washington famous in the colonies, and in England as well for the journal was printed and read with great curiosity in London.

On February 21 the Virginia House of Burgesses voted the sum of £50 to Major George Washington "to testify our Approbation of his Proceedings on his Journey to the *Ohio.*"

This mission given to an obscure youth who bravely carried it out against overwhelming odds in an unknown corner of the world led to the French and Indian War, a new future for Canada, and, eventually, to the American Revolution which has affected the course of history to this very day.

The famous American writer Washington Irving wrote a hundred years after this journey that Washington's mission and surviving its hardships "all pointed him out, not merely to the governor, but to the public at large, as one eminently fitted, not withstanding his youth, for important trust involving civil as well as military duties. It is an expedition that may be considered the foundation of his fortunes. From that moment he was the rising hope of Virginia."

Glossary

Allegheny Mountains part of the Appalachian Mountain range in Pennsylvania, Maryland, and western Virginia.

Anteroom small waiting room outside a larger room.

Axis central dividing line.

Bark house house made out of tree branches covered with bark pulled off of trees.

Calumet long-stemmed pipe with elaborate decorations that North American Indians used to smoke tobacco or leaves on ceremonial occasions. Sometimes called a peace pipe.

Council group of people appointed or elected to give advice.

Dialects various ways of speaking the same basic language.

Esquire title of courtesy that refers to a man considered to be a gentleman.

Gaol eighteenth-century word for jail.

Great house	Indian name for a frontier fort.
Hominy cake	small bread- or pancake-like food made of corn.
Indentured servant	individual who agreed to work for someone, usually for a period of seven years, in payment of a debt.
Iroquois League	six Indian tribes or nations—Mohawks, Oneidas, Onondagas, Cayugas, Senecas, and Tuscaroras—who joined together into a confederacy.
League	about three miles.
Lean-to	three-sided shed with a steeply slanting roof.
Longhouse	bark house up to 100 feet long in which several Indian families belonging to the same clan lived together.
Militia	citizen-soldiers used only in emergencies usually to defend their hometown or colony.
Ocher	yellow pigment with which the Indians painted their faces.
Portage	travel overland between two bodies of water.

Queue	man's hair caught at the back of the neck with a band or thin ribbon.
Shining Mountains	the Rocky Mountains.
Spirits	strong liquor.
Surveyor	someone who determines the boundaries of land through measuring and mathematics.
Viands	food.
Wigwam	round hut consisting of poles covered with bark or animal skins.